HERE'S WHAT PEOPLE ARE
BRANDEN BRIM
COURAGE: A MESSAGE FROM HEAVEN...

My friend Branden Brim has written a book that you won't want to put down until you've read it cover to cover! His personal testimonies and revelations from God will help you overcome obstacles and receive new victories in the midst of trials that have been standing in your way. With the state of the world right now, there's no doubt that this book is an important prophetic message for today! I especially appreciate Branden's willingness to openly write about his glorious heavenly vision, sharing the supernatural encounter he had with the biblical King David in a way that empowers the reader with fresh insight and deeper hunger for the things of God. I believe that this book will leave a lasting impartation with those who are yielded and ready to embark on a spiritual journey into receiving divine courage from the glory realm. Open wide your heart as you read!

—*Joshua Mills*
Co-founder, International Glory Ministries
Bestselling author, *Power Portals* and *Creative Glory*

To go along with the ways of the world is expected, but to go against the grain takes courage. As a friend to both Branden and Destanie Brim, I can confidently say that they are trendsetters for believers across the globe.

—*Colton Dixon*
Musician and songwriter

Some people never reach their full potential and complete the mission or plan God has for their life. Many times, it can be attributed to the lack of one key ingredient: courage. In his new book, *Courage: A Message from Heaven*, Branden Brim answers the questions of how to find the courage to maintain focus on the goal, even through the hardships of life. I have known Branden since he was very young. He was raised to be strong in faith and how to hear from God. I observed the intensity of the calling on his life, even in his younger years, and watched as he has grown deep in the revelation of God's Word. You can trust him to hear from heaven. Branden walks courageously in his ministry, teaching the Word. I would highly recommend that you listen to what he has to say and apply the principles contained about courage. This book is a life-changer.

—*Dr. Larry Ollison*
Larry Ollison Ministries

If there was a book for the times we are living in, this is it! The world seems to be spinning out of control in many areas unlike anything we've ever seen before. This book is like a guide to help you navigate through the ever-changing culture we are facing in our lives every day. It takes courage to stand up and "run toward the problem rather than fleeing," as Branden puts it. His unique delivery is like a fresh wind in a time we need it most. This truly is a message from heaven.

—*RayGene Wilson*
Pastor, West Coast Life Church, Murrieta, CA

Courage is strength in the face of pain or grief. Branden Brim brings us a very timely word of strength, healing, and hope, speaking into the heart of this generation. This comes from a young man who has dedicated himself to touching the hearts of people. As you read these pages, your heart will come alive with faith to overcome the obstacles in life, a very inspiring word in this hour.

—*Dr. E. Daniel Ponce, D.D., B.Th.*
Presiding bishop, United With Christ Ministries

An encounter with heavenly realities will change anyone who will put them to work. Like Gideon of old, who went from a fearful, downtrodden, cowardly man to a mighty man of valor and courage, I believe this generation of believers is heading toward a mighty encounter with God that will also bring great transformation, courage, and boldness to shake the world with God's glory before the coming of the Lord. Branden Brim has been called, anointed, appointed, and prepared by the Lord to be at the forefront of this courageous new generation of believers. His heavenly lessons on courage change and transform him. I believe they will also change you as you read his experience and wisdom in this powerful book.

—*Julio E. Hernández, B.Th. MCC*
United With Christ Ministries

There are two phases of life, and Branden is in that first phase of being young, having energy, and being willing to take risks that others would not, loving God, and having the courage to go where others might not go. As a member of the second phase of life, Branden, I have great love and respect for you and have enjoyed watching you emerge as a symbol of courage and grace to your generation. You have crafted an indispensable book on courage, a message that must be launched into a culture that is riddled with fear and anxiety. Though you are young, you have proven your value in God's army, and I believe your book will be a source of motivation for many.

—Don Milam
Publishing and writing consultant
Author, *The Ancient Language of Eden*

Once in a while, an author comes your way, and what he is saying is just the right word for this time in your life. *Courage* is the word that Branden Brim has for us today. In this book, you will see yourself in a whole new light and know you were created to overcome in all areas of life. *Courage: A Message from Heaven* will cause you to come up to a new place in your walk with God. I know that while you are reading this book, you will rise up in your heart and say, "I can do this. I can overcome." Branden shares his stories of courage and moments in his life. Grab a cup of hot coffee or tea, sit back, and let this timely book help you to be courageous. You will be glad you did. Enjoy!

—Rick Reyna
Founder, Rally Ministry

Branden Brim's new book *Courage: A Message from Heaven* is truly a godsend for the hour we are living in. I believe each reader will be set free from the opinions and desires of man and in turn be fully surrendered to God. I also believe that this book will challenge you to take courageous steps toward walking into your destiny and the plan of God for your life.

—*Joseph Harris*
Lead pastor, Love Center Church MD & LA

Branden has been given a tremendous revelation of what it looks like to have courage for the days ahead. While the world is in great turmoil and crisis, those who have the courage to use their authority through faith in Jesus's name will experience one of the greatest outpourings of the Holy Spirit to usher in the end-time harvest. Branden has been raised up as a standard for this very moment in history to push back the flood of darkness and shine bright for all those who both see and hear the exploits of faith in his life and ministry—a firebrand for Jesus! I believe this book will impact you in such a way that you will run like never before with the fire of God to destroy every ungodly thing you face that tries to discourage you until our Savior returns for His blood-bought church. Thank you, Branden, for sharing your message from heaven with the world. May we all be found with courage in these last hours of daylight before the Lord's return.

—*Pastor Allyn Clevenger*
FaithLife Olympia Church
Clevenger Ministries International

This is not your typical book on courage and faith. *Courage: A Message from Heaven* is exactly what the name communicates. It is a Holy Ghost-anointed message from heaven. It is fun to read, insightful, biblically based, and a must read in these final moments of the end of days. Branden Brim's life experience and a true heavenly vision the Lord allowed Branden to experience will resound in your spirit. Branden and Destanie Brim don't just speak about courage, they live it! I give this book my highest endorsement as I do Branden Brim and his ministry. This book is a blueprint from heaven for Christian courage.

—*Tim Henderson*
Pastor, Jonathan Creek Fellowship, Sullivan, IL

Since first hearing Branden share this message on courage, which he received through a heavenly vision, it has made a profound impact on my life. Courage equips us to advance, possess new territory, and overcome any obstacle in our life that seems impossible. I believe this is a timely message for the body of Christ today!

—*ReJeanna Jolliff*
ReJeanna Jolliff Ministries

Being Branden's brother, I have been a witness to the encounters and experiences that he is writing about. These stories are true and I stand by every word. What this book covers only scratches the surface of encounters he and our family have had with the Lord, including various spiritual things. I was with him, watching him work through life's various trials and tribulations. During these times, it seemed like there was no way out. These were hard times on us all. And I watched as the Lord took Branden from this low place and lifted him up miraculously through victory while being shrouded with humility. I'm so proud of Branden and his willingness to trust the Lord and do it when no one else understood him, obeying God's word, seeing the goodness of God for himself, and setting an example we should all live by.

—*Jared Houle*
Brand specialist, Billye Brim Ministries

It's amazing to see the spiritual growth in my brother and his hunger to be used of God. After Branden had his heavenly encounter, I remember the courage and boldness that came out of him. He was completely transformed. We are living in an hour that requires us to walk in courage. I believe that people reading this book will be completely changed by a fresh impartation of heavenly courage to fulfill God's plan for their lives.

—*Hannah Brim*
Hannah Brim Ministries

COURAGE

A MESSAGE FROM HEAVEN

BRANDEN BRIM

WHITAKER
HOUSE

COURAGE
A Message from Heaven

His Name Ministries
P.O. Box 262
Montclair, CA 91763
www.hisnameministries.com
www.facebook.com/HisNameMinistries
www.instagram.com/hisnameministries
twitter.com/brandenbrim

ISBN: 978-1-64123-859-5
eBook ISBN: 978-1-64123-860-1
Printed in the United States of America
© 2022 by Branden Brim

Whitaker House
1030 Hunt Valley Circle
New Kensington, PA 15068
www.whitakerhouse.com

Library of Congress Control Number: 2022935065

1 2 3 4 5 6 7 8 9 10 11 **WI** 29 28 27 26 25 24 23 22

CONTENTS

FOREWORD

When my grandson, Branden Brim, was caught up to heaven to learn about courage at age twenty-three, he was facing a difficult decision that would affect the God-given life's path he was to walk.

Before Branden's "catching away," the Lord was dealing with him about having the courage to make that decision. "Courage" Scriptures were brought to his mind. One day while he was lying down, meditating upon those Scriptures, angels appeared over him. They put thin layers of heavenly substance, layer upon layer, into his chest area. He felt power go into him. Eventually, he was caught away into a classroom in heaven. He shares more detail in this book, but I'll only say here that the class was on "Courage," and King David was the teacher.

Then Branden was in another classroom. The teacher was quite different—evidently an elder, with a long white beard, wearing long, flowing clothing. A huge Bible was before him. The class was on "Numbers in Scripture." Branden thought, *This is a class more suited for my grandmother.* I would certainly have liked to be in that classroom!

When Branden told me about this experience, I immediately remembered a trip to Israel, and the importance of the Hebrew word *derekh*. Our Israeli guide told my pastor son, Chip, "You Christians don't see Proverbs 22:6 the way we do."

Proverbs 22:6 says, "*Train up a child in the way* [derekh] *he should go, and when he is old he will not depart from it.*"

The guide went on to say that each of us has a life's path or *derekh* that the Lord has designed for us to walk. And Jews believe they are to help their children discover that path and train for it. Many Scriptures teach us we are each given a *derekh*. Courage is an essential attribute in order to discover and walk one's particular *derekh*. Branden's revelation will help you discover and walk your *derekh* pleasing to the Father.

—*Dr. Billye Brim*
Billye Brim Ministries

INTRODUCTION

Courage is contagious. When a brave man takes a
stand, the spines of others are often stiffened.
—*Billy Graham*

In the deepest forests of Ecuador lived a tribe that was known
to be violent and dangerous. When missionary Jim Elliot heard
about the Aucas, it tugged at his heart. He was determined to
lead them to Christ.

He put together a team of four men, and on January 6, 1956,
they succeeded in meeting an Auca man and two women. The
missionaries praised God for this encounter and made plans to
visit the entire tribe. But when they returned two days later,
they were massacred—martyred for Jesus.

Jim's short life, filled with the desire to share God's love, can
be summed up by something he wrote in his journal: "He is no

fool who gives what he cannot keep to gain that which he cannot lose."[1] Courageously, the five missionaries sacrificed their lives for the cause of Christ.

Courage is necessary for the followers of Christ. Commonly defined, courage means being motivated from the heart to do something brave. The *Merriam-Webster Dictionary* describes courage as "mental or moral strength to venture, persevere, and withstand danger, fear, or difficulty." As believers, we can have the courage, boldness, and guts to believe in God for the impossible, or when we walk in dangerous places. With courage, we can face everyday situations as a victor instead of a victim.

WITH COURAGE, WE CAN FACE EVERYDAY SITUATIONS AS A VICTOR INSTEAD OF A VICTIM.

It is a lesson I earned from my personal experiences, and I believe it is just as powerful now as it was for me initially. I grew up in a Christian home, a part of a ministry family. Eventually, I met and married my beautiful wife Destanie, and later, we were led to go into full-time ministry. Through His Name Ministries—a name we chose because of the power we have in the name of Jesus—we traveled all around the world, sharing the gospel everywhere we went. As our ministry grew, I started to reflect on my past life. In those early days of ministry,

1. Madeline Peña, "Jim and Elisabeth Elliot: Devotion to the Unreached," Bethany Global University (bethanygu.edu/blog/stories/jim-and-elisabeth-elliot).

I didn't know my purpose in life, let alone what it meant to be courageous.

But there I was, preaching boldly to people all across the globe. I could never have done this in the past! How did it happen?

I believe one encounter with God can change someone's life forever, and that is precisely what happened to me. I clearly remember the time God showed me the vision of an extraordinary class in heaven. The course subject was courage, and the instructor was King David. That one encounter made me the man I am today.

Quite a long time ago, God told me to write this book on courage. In John 2:5, Jesus's mother told the servants at the wedding feast in Cana, *"Whatever He says to you, do it."* And since He told me to write this book, I have done so. I pray that what I have written will enable you to live a life full of courage and boldness. I hope that from this day forward, you will never be the same!

Are you ready?

1

COURAGE WITH PURPOSE

Look up! Take courage! Jesus has shaken the
foundations of death and darkness.
He fights for you and there is none like Him.
—*Smith Wigglesworth*

What is courage, and what is its source? How do you get it when you need it? What prevents you from cowering in a cave for security when danger lurks?

Courage is a deliberate choice and willingness to confront suffering, agony, risk, the threat of death, hardship, uncertainty, or intimidation. Moral courage is the ability to respond rightly in the face of widespread opposition and popular opinion.

In his article "The Emotions of Courage," Professor Daniel Putman writes:

The ideal in courage is not just a rigid control of fear, nor is it a denial of the emotion. The ideal is to judge a situation, accept the emotion as part of human nature and, we hope, use well-developed habits to confront the fear and allow reason to guide our behavior toward a worthwhile goal.[2]

The Bible is full of stories of men and women mightily used by God in the face of physical peril and bitter opposition. They all share common threads: the people showed strength in adversity and loyalty to God and His purposes. Courageous people loyal to God aren't afraid to face giants or challenge hostile enemies. Rather than fleeing, they run toward the problem.

THE CALL FOR COURAGE

Compared to those who sacrificed much and endured considerable hardships, many Christians today forfeit little and suffer nothing for the cause of Christ. What happened to all of that courage? Why do we not see demonstrations of courage in our churches?

Jesus spoke with boldness, and we should be imitators of Him. After He taught in the temple, some people said:

*But look! He speaks **boldly**, and they say nothing to Him. Do the rulers know indeed that this is truly the Christ?*
(John 7:26)

With great freedom and courage, openly and publicly, Jesus boldly spoke in the temple, holding nothing back. And the religious leaders said nothing to Him; they did not contradict Him,

---

2. Daniel Putman, "The Emotions of Courage" *Journal of Social Philosophy* 32, no. 4 (2001): 465.

nor did they prohibit Him from speaking. With great liberty, Jesus accused the Jews of conspiring to kill Him, confronting them with the truth that infuriated them.

The author of Hebrews, in chapter eleven, describes the hall of faith as men and women who, through faith:

> *Escaped the edge of the sword, out of weakness were made strong, became valiant in battle, turned to flight the armies of the aliens. Women received their dead raised to life again. Others were tortured, not accepting deliverance...They were stoned, they were sawn in two, were tempted, were slain with the sword. They wandered about in sheepskins and goatskins, being destitute, afflicted, tormented—of whom the world was not worthy. They wandered in deserts and mountains, in dens and caves of the earth. And all these, having obtained a good testimony through faith.*
>
> (Hebrews 11:34–39)

In the last generations, many men and women were willing to sacrifice everything to spread the message of Christ in the world's dangerous places, where many pioneers died from cancer or were killed by cannibals. Others like Richard Wurmbrand, who wrote the book *Tortured for Christ*, endured much for the sake of the gospel.

BOLD AS A LION, STEADY AS OUR ROCK

What should be our response in our generation? The correct response is to have courage and put our complete trust in God, especially in these last days, doing all we can to advance God's kingdom at all costs. Be bold as a lion and steady as our Rock, Jesus.

The wicked flee when no one pursues, but the righteous are **bold as a lion.** (Proverbs 28:1)

Blessed be **the Lord my Rock,** *Who trains my hands for war, and my fingers for battle.* (Psalm 144:1)

In the Acts of the Apostles, Peter and John demonstrated that Jesus was not dead but alive and operating through them to rock the world with the kingdom message. They paid the price and experienced torture, imprisonment, beatings, and death. The religious leaders thought they were done with Jesus, having negotiated His crucifixion with Pilate. But to their surprise, He rose from the dead and was now living through Peter and John, who demonstrated the same boldness as their master.

Now when they saw the boldness of Peter and John, and perceived that they were uneducated and untrained men, they marveled. And they realized that they had been with Jesus. (Acts 4:13)

The first-century church grew by faith amid persecution and suffering. In our generation, in the suffering church, Christians are harassed, arrested, interrogated, imprisoned, fined, or killed because of their religious beliefs and practices, yet the church flourishes. Nelson Mandela learned that courage is not the absence of fear but the triumph over it. The brave man is not he who does not feel afraid, but he who conquers that fear.

We might not be suffering in the Western world like those in other countries, but we face opposition and ridicule in the schools and wherever we go. Every day, people are faced with opportunities to live by faith, even when it's scary. We have opportunities to manifest courage in difficult places. The church must create a culture of courage, encouraging people to take advantage of opportunities for change. During times of accelerated change and uncertainty, anxiety increases, and the courage to take risks diminishes. Yet, these are the times and seasons to make the boldest action, allowing you to advance God's kingdom. We can do so in ways both big and small.

THE BRAVE MAN IS NOT HE WHO DOES NOT FEEL AFRAID, BUT HE WHO CONQUERS THAT FEAR.

On one occasion, I was with my family in a coffee shop. We were enjoying each other's company, and I was sipping my usual drink, iced coffee with just a little bit of ice and cream, when I spotted a friend of mine who had just walked through the door. The coffee shop was busy that night, with crowds of people around every table. As I walked over to chat with my friend, I decided I would buy a coffee for him.

CARRYING HIS PRESENCE

While I was paying for his drink, I noticed my friend was stuttering and giving me a funny look. I didn't pay much attention to this; we talked for a bit and eventually, we said our goodbyes. Shortly after leaving the coffee shop, I received a text message from my friend, who said he was happy to see me and thanked me for the coffee. Then the conversation shifted to the reason for his odd behavior. He told me that as we were talking in the coffee shop, he saw Jesus on me. It surprised him, and he didn't know how to respond.

I've had this happen quite often, and I pray that you experience it, too. People need to see Jesus in you. When you are in God's presence, you become saturated in the glory. It happened with Moses, and the sons of Israel saw the glory on his face. (See Exodus 34:29–30.) Experiences like that stir my heart and constantly remind me of the need to live in His presence. I believe it pleases Jesus when we gaze upon His face and carry His presence with us.

Even though I'm a young minister, I have faced obstacles and encountered attacks from the enemy. Instead of fixating on those things, I focus on Jesus. I know I can depend on Him for courage even in the most trying times. It reminds me how blessed I am to have been raised in a Christian home and to do ministry with family.

A VOICE, NOT AN ECHO

My grandmother, Dr. Billye Brim, is a well-known minister who preaches the Word in her travels and on her TV show, *The Prophetic Witness*. Her ministry headquarters is Prayer Mountain in the Ozarks, located in Branson, Missouri. She also has a church near Tulsa, Oklahoma, and even has property in Israel, where she plans to build a prayer and study center.

It seems like everyone in my family can preach! A typical Brim family gathering goes like this: we see each other, there are hugs and laughs all around, and then one of my family members tells us what God is doing in their life. Another jumps in, telling us what they hear God saying. The times we share are such blessings, and I thank God for them!

However, even though I was brought up in a beautiful Christian home, I had to develop my relationship with God. I hope you realize that Jesus wants to know *you* in a more profound and personal way, too. Albert Einstein once said, "Be a voice, not an echo." Don't just mindlessly repeat what you've heard and blindly follow others, but speak from your knowledge and experience. You can either be a leader or a follower, an originator or imitator. It's your choice. An echo just repeats a fact, but a voice *knows* the fact. That's a big difference!

GOD WANTS US TO KNOW HIM WITH OUR HEARTS.

Faith is believing in your heart and speaking with your mouth. (See Mark 11:22.) God said that He wants us to know Him with our hearts. We live in a church culture where many people are echoes, repeating what others say, but do not have the experience. They may say that Jesus is alive, that Jesus is a healer, and that Jesus loves them. They might say they're blessed with favor, but they don't truly believe it, and the end result is that they experience defeated lives. There is no power in what they say, and people won't listen to them.

Marinate yourself in the Word. Allow it to sink deep into your heart, embrace it by faith, and begin to declare it over yourself daily. It may start as an echo, but eventually, you will become a voice.

John G. Lake believed in the power of understanding *Christ in you* and wrote these words:

> Christ's indwelling in the human heart is the mystery of mysteries. Paul gave it to the Gentiles as the supreme mystery of God's revelation and the finality of all wonder he knew. *"Christ in you"* (Colossians 1:27). Christ has a purpose in you. Christ's purpose in you is to reveal Himself to you, through you, in you. We repeat over and over that familiar phrase *"the church, which is His body"* (Ephesians 1:22–23), but if we realized the truth of it and the power of it, this world would be a different place. When the Christian church realizes that they are the tangible, living, pulsating flesh and bones and blood and brain of Jesus Christ, and that God is manifesting Himself through each one every minute and is endeavoring to accomplish His big will for the world through them, not through some other body, then Christian responsibility would be understood. Jesus Christ operates through you. He does not operate independently of you. He operates through you. Man and God become united. That is the divine secret of a real Christian life.[3]

Christ is in *you*.

---

3. John G. Lake, *The Flow of the Spirit: Divine Secrets of a Real Christian Life* (New Kensington, PA: Whitaker House, 2018), 149–150.

LIFE IS A TEST

No matter what your age or occupation, every day, you are tested with unforeseen challenges. You either accept these challenges and meet them head-on, or resist them and try to wish them away. Yet challenges are intertwined with the fabric of our lives. They are the tests we face daily.

There was a time when I was just an echo. I knew all the right church words to say, but the words were lifeless. As I write this book on courage, I can honestly tell you that this subject came alive because of the experiences on my journey. I was forced to live life by courage every day, and the times of testing caused me to grow up quickly. God always knows how our life circumstances will affect us, but we don't.

My challenge came when I was asked to fill a vacant position, with the opportunity to travel, with my grandmother in her ministry.

I was excited to become her personal assistant, helping her any way I could, such as setting up the book and CD table. At the time, I had no idea what the full extent of my duties would be, nor how vital this position would be to my spiritual growth and fellowship with God. But God knew, as He always does.

He knew precisely what I needed and was preparing me for what was to come. Those first few trips were great, but I wasn't yet entirely on fire for God. That change came over time.

Don't get me wrong. I loved Jesus, and I read my Bible, but He didn't occupy the first place in my life at all. God wasn't my priority yet. I was still doing ungodly things like listening to music and media that didn't bring Him glory and talking to people who were not so godly. I had relationships with the wrong girls. I was only concerned about myself during that time.

Once, we traveled on a ministry tour to Canada; the meeting schedule stretched more than a month and took us all over that beautiful country. My grandmother was part of a huge conference in Ottawa. When we arrived at the convention center, we headed to the back green room, where the other ministers were gathering. As we were about to walk into the room, my grandmother said, "Branden, the other minister speaking at this conference is a powerful man of God and full of the Holy Spirit."

I told her, "Thank you for telling me," while silently repenting. I didn't want any Spirit-filled minister walking by, trying to confront me and tell me what I was doing wrong. I asked Jesus to wash me and cleanse me from anything that was not of Him, ending with, "In Jesus's name, amen."

So, we walked into the room, and the minister seemed to be drawn to me like a magnet. He locked eyes with me, walked straight over to me, and said, "Let's go on a walk." As we did so, the minister spoke to me and prayed with me. It was a momentous occasion, and yet that is only one encounter with God that affected me and my future.

While I faithfully carried out my duties for my grandmother, I was often dismayed by her requests for me to speak at meetings. We would be on our way to a church service, and she would tell me, "Branden, I want you to share in the meeting and tell them what God has shown you." It was like a punch in the gut because I didn't feel prepared and wasn't in a place to preach. I was not even thinking about that opportunity, but God was!

I can see more clearly now how God was preparing me the whole time. Trusting God, I agreed to minister publicly. I was not alone, for the Holy Spirit helped me and ministered to people through me. They were sometimes overwhelmed by God's presence. Though I was a novice in ministry and sounded nervous when I spoke, I didn't let that affect me. I knew God was doing something special in my life, and if I cried in front of people because I sensed God's presence, then so be it!

JESUS IS MORE THAN A SERMON PREACHED OR A BIBLE LESSON TAUGHT. HE IS THE SOURCE OF LIFE WITHIN YOU, INFUSED WITH HIS LOVE AND POWER.

My life was changing dramatically. I was experiencing God in a way I never knew before. I went from being lukewarm to being on fire for God. It was beyond anything I had ever known, and it was amazing. Jesus was more than a sermon preached or a Bible lesson taught. He became the source of life within me, a life that infused me with His love and power. I was sensing it all the time. Daily, I felt Him pouring love into me, changing me by the minute. The things holding me back, the bad habits, the way I talked, and the emotions out of whack were all melting away by His love.

Everyone I knew saw the change in me, and I didn't say a word about it. People saw Jesus in me, just as the early church saw Jesus in Peter and John. One man I had known my whole life didn't recognize me. Walking in God's love and living in God's presence made the difference.

MARRIAGE AND MOVING

After three years of traveling and serving as a personal assistant to my grandmother, I met my future wife Destanie at a church conference. She was talking to my sister Hannah, but I only said a few words to her. Although I felt a spark, I wasn't anxious to find a wife and get married. I wasn't looking for a wife either; I was seeking God to know His will for me. I knew the Lord would bring my wife to me when the time was right, so I was not worried about it.

I mentioned to Destanie that I would be in California on a ministry trip. After I arrived there, she reached out to me on social media. We started hanging out together with her family and one of my relatives—and the rest is history. Now I know that God put Destanie in my life. That feeling grew from the first time we met until we got married nine months later. Yes, we moved fast, but we knew it was God.

At the same time, I sensed the Holy Spirit saying, "Move to California!" Was I hearing God right? Move to California? You would think it wasn't the best decision in the natural, leaving the job that provided security and income, not to mention my family. Knowing God called me to preach, I thought the best way to flourish would be to stay with my grandmother and have the opportunity to meet pastors and other key leaders. But no, God called me to move to California and to trust Him. Making that decision required buckets of courage to trust God in the face of what appeared to be impossible and maybe even insane.

The path required abandoning the natural way of thinking and embracing the spiritual.

> *But the natural man does not receive the things of the Spirit of God, for they are foolishness to him; nor can he know them, because they are spiritually discerned.*
>
> (1 Corinthians 2:14)

To the world, such a decision might look like a hasty, immature choice, but I leaned on the Spirit for the right decision, and I knew what it was: go to California!

I didn't need to look for any man to open the way for us because I believed that if God had called me, He would open the way. The Lord is our Way Maker. God told me, "Make the right decision, be courageous, and move to California." The path was fixed, and I was at peace.

My family blessed me the night before my trip to California. We were all at my grandmother's home with other well-known ministers, and everyone prayed for me before sending me off. Among the ministers there was my spiritual father, Dr. Gary Wood. He was a powerful preacher with an amazing testimony about being supernaturally raised from the dead after a fatal car accident when he was a young man.[4]

The night before I left, Dr. Wood told me, "Branden, I prayed Psalm 91 over you, asking for angels to watch over you and keep you on your way to California, in Jesus's name. Amen!"

(In my beginning years of ministry, before Dr. Wood died a second time and returned to heaven forever, my wife and I traveled with him, praying and opening each service before

4. Dr. Gary L. Wood, *I Saw the Glories of Heaven: A Story of Healing, Hope, and Life after Death* (New Kensington, PA: Whitaker House, 2018).

preaching. We saw many miracles and supernatural manifestations everywhere we went.)

I left my grandmother's house and went back home to prepare for my drive the next morning. I woke up early, and my little red Honda was packed with everything I owned: some clothes, a Bible, and barely any money. Was I scared? Yes, I was, but I knew I was obeying God, and I spoke courage into my soul: "Branden, you have courage. Holy Spirit, give me courage." Part of me didn't want to leave, but I chose to obey the voice of Jesus.

Before driving off, I went back into the house and ran down the stairs to tell my mom goodbye and tell her that I loved her. She was startled to see me, saying, "I thought you had already left." She had seen a vision, she said, and would tell me about it later.

After my mom held me tight and prayed for me, I got in my car and began the long drive to California. A little later, feeling a bit curious, I called my mom and asked her what she saw.

"Branden," she said, "at about six in the morning, an angel walked into my room and looked at me. And he looked like you, and I heard him talking about different things. I knew he was sent to help you on your trip to California."

This was the very thing that Dr. Wood had prayed for the night before.

I sensed the angel with me in my car, assisting me and protecting me on my trip. It was the most peaceful and most leisurely drive I have ever experienced. I believe God answered my prayer for courage and even allowed my mom to see the angel to encourage her. Angels are "all ministering spirits sent forth *to minister for those who will inherit salvation"* (Hebrews 1:14). That's us!

A NEW BEGINNING

When I arrived in California, I was excited to see what God would do in my life and through my ministry. I imagined God had plans for me to travel again like I did with my grandmother, meeting powerful men and women of God and going to some of the biggest churches.

But my first day in California was nothing like I expected; it wasn't glamorous at all. I was going to live in a small trailer on a property owned by Destanie's family—and my first job was to wax the trailer! Instead of being an incredible preacher before large crowds, I was waxing an old trailer for several days. Talk about humility! I sensed a desire to quit and return home. I felt like I had marched back one hundred steps from the place of ministry I knew. In my heart, I said, "God, why this?"

Then, in my spirit, I heard the Lord speaking to me. "Branden, I didn't come to be served; I came to serve."

As always, God's presence busted me and encouraged me to trust Him during this time. As the refrain of an old hymn goes, "Trust and obey, for there's no other way."[5] I decided to volunteer by helping Rally Ministry, founded by Destanie's parents, in any way possible. When I wasn't helping, I was crying in my small trailer, asking God for His help but mostly spending time with Him. A season in the secret place became a lifestyle in that place of His presence. In that secret place with God, I was building a platform for courageous living.

---

5. "Trust and Obey" by John H. Sammis (1887).

Two months after arriving in California, I married Destanie, and we ended up living in that small trailer together. I was a bit surprised when people sent offerings to my grandmother's ministry designated for me. No one knew what I was doing, but God did, and He was speaking to people's hearts about us—so much so that after one year, we had received three times the amount I had made working full-time in Missouri. We serve a supernatural God! I was young but learning fast that God truly does work in mysterious ways.

DON'T LOOK TO MAN FOR BREAKTHROUGHS AND MIRACLES—TRUST GOD AND DO WHAT HE TELLS YOU TO DO.

Don't look to man for breakthroughs and miracles—trust God and do what He tells you to do. I am not looking for a way when Jesus *is* the Way. He will prepare the way, opening doors that no man can open! Our ministry began with a call to preach, and I shared my heart with God. "You called me to preach," I told Him, "and You will open the right doors for me. I won't sell myself for meetings and making partners for ministry. You are the Way Maker and the door buster!"

Every night, I would preach a message to myself in front of a mirror. That little trailer became my church for preaching to myself, and I did it with enthusiasm. I was exercising and preparing for the future and what God was planting in my heart.

As I preached enthusiastically in that small trailer while looking in the mirror, it built courage in me. Faith was filling my heart as I shared from the Word of God.

Every year, our ministry grew by leaps and bounds, with the best only from Him and doing what He called us to do. We have an extensive partner base now, and I am thankful to God for how He uses them to support us and our ministry. Despite our lack of courage to launch out on our own without a little support initially, God was faithful. Even when I was discouraged or felt like quitting, I pressed forward and always prayed for more courage. Courage is releasing the familiar to discover the future that awaits you as God leads you.

2

BE COURAGEOUS; TAKE A CHANCE

Have courage and believe that God will hear and help.
We are waiting on a God who could
never disappoint His people.
—*Andrew Murray*

After Scottish missionary Mary Slessor traveled to West Africa in the late 1800s, she became a renowned figure of her time while serving God in Nigeria. For forty years, she served as an evangelist and teacher who fought against social injustice and tribal infanticide. She was one of the first single missionary women to make a worldwide impact.

Mary was born in 1848, the second of seven children in a poor and troubled home. Although her mother was deeply religious, her father was an alcoholic who brought the family to abject poverty, fear, and misery. Mary worked twelve hours a day to help support her family and also taught Sunday school, evangelizing street children.

While attending church with her mother and siblings, Mary heard the stories of famous missionaries. She was especially attracted to the life of David Livingstone. She read about his travels, his fight against slavery in Africa, his treks deep into the heart of the continent, and how he won cannibals over to Christ.

Livingstone became Mary's hero. She was captivated as she read about his courageous and lonely life. When he died, she heard his words in her heart: "I go to Africa to try to make an open door....; do you carry out the work which I have begun. I LEAVE IT WITH YOU."[6]

That sealed the deal. Mary was determined to follow in Livingstone's footsteps and become a missionary in Africa.

At age twenty-nine, Mary Slessor arrived in Calabar, Nigeria. She was initially assigned to work in a city school with other European missionaries, but her heart was set on doing pioneer work among unreached people. Other missionaries spoke of the "savagery" and "heathenness" of such people, but that was precisely where Mary felt the gospel needed to be lived and proclaimed. Mary was born with courage in her blood and was determined to go where no one else would go.

Four years later, she was able to move out into a tribal area. Deciding to live with the local people as they lived, she moved into a traditional African house. As she settled in, identifying with the people she had come to serve became a core value.

---

6. Basil Mathews, *The Book of Missionary Heroes* (New York: George H. Doran Company, 1922); www.gutenberg.org/files/16657/16657-h/16657-h.htm.

Indeed, Mary's close identification with the people and her living out the gospel among them enabled her to be instrumental in settling tribal hostilities. She successfully battled witch doctors' "healing" practices and fought other methods contrary to God's design. For example, she convinced one tribe to give up their practice of killing infant twins. She was so respected and influential that she came to be called "the white queen of Calabar."

For the last four decades of her life, Mary suffered intermittent fevers from malaria she had contracted during her first station to Calabar. However, she downplayed the personal costs and never gave up her mission work. The fevers eventually weakened her to the point where she could no longer walk long distances in the rainforest but had to be pushed along in a handcart. In January 1915, while at her remote station, she suffered a particularly severe fever, and God called her home. Throughout her life and ministry, whenever Mary faced a decision, she consistently chose the path that placed her firmly in God's will, despite the cost.

FINDING SECURITY AND COURAGE IN GOD'S WILL

I, too, had a choice on which direction I could take for my life. I would have been more secure had I remained with my grandmother, but I chose to go to California with no support. I had hardly any money, but I had faith and courage, knowing I was obeying God by doing His will for my life. I discovered that the most secure place in the world is living in the center of God's will.

The word "will" carries the idea of purpose and design. Purpose plus design equals the will of God. God has a purpose for our lives, and purpose is revealed in God's design for your life. When you live your life for Him, you are proving that His will is good, acceptable, and perfect.

> *And do not be conformed to this world, but be transformed by the renewing of your mind, that you may prove what is that good and acceptable and perfect **will of God.***
>
> (Romans 12:2)

If you investigate the will of God, you will discover that God's way is higher than ours, and His will is fitted perfectly for our lives. The Greek word for "will" is *thélō*, which means "wish," "desire," and "intention." It is an imitation of the Hebrew word *chaphets*, which means "to take delight" and "have pleasure."

DO NOT RESIST GOD'S WILL BUT TAKE DELIGHT AND PLEASURE IN HIS DESIGNED PLANS FOR YOUR LIFE.

Do not resist God's will but take delight and pleasure in His designed plans for your life. Indeed, there are times when His plan will lead you to places requiring courage.

You are no longer a stranger but a member of God's household, and in Ephesians 2:20, Paul refers to Jesus as *"the chief cornerstone."* He is our sure foundation. In Christ, we find the courage to be what He called us to become. While some dare to die as martyrs for the gospel, others don't dare to talk about Jesus to people.

Courage comes in different packages. Malala Yousafzai, a young Pakistani activist, was shot because she spoke up for the education of girls. Every day, firefighters rush into burning buildings. Some people exhibit courage in obvious and visible ways, but all of us can exhibit courage. It involves training ourselves to perform small, daily acts of bravery, and this training helps you grow in your courage. *Courage means being afraid and acting anyway.*

Most of us were not born courageous, so we shouldn't expect to acquire it magically without practice. Brené Brown, author of *The Gifts of Imperfection*, says faith "is a place of mystery, where we find the courage to believe in what we cannot see and the strength to let go of our fear of uncertainty." Courage, she says, "gives us a voice, and compassion gives us an ear."

THE GOOD FIGHT ISN'T ALWAYS EASY

We can always use more courage; it is a process of growth. Paul told young Timothy to *"fight the good fight of faith"* (1 Timothy 6:12). *"For God has not given us a spirit of fear, but of power and of love and of a sound mind"* (2 Timothy 1:7).

Lester Sumrall, a mighty man of God who now is in heaven, exemplified what it meant to have courage. He once said, "You are either going to dominate the devil, or he is going to dominate you." That's so true; it's one or the other. We must have courage and boldness to *"fight the good fight of faith."* Dominating the devil and using your authority over him is the courageous path to victory, while allowing the enemy to dominate you results in oppression and hopelessness.

DOMINATING THE DEVIL AND USING YOUR AUTHORITY OVER HIM IS THE COURAGEOUS PATH TO VICTORY, WHILE ALLOWING THE ENEMY TO DOMINATE YOU RESULTS IN OPPRESSION AND HOPELESSNESS.

Every morning, I read Paul's prayerful epistle to the church at Ephesus, starting with Ephesians 1:15–23. Next, I read Ephesians 2:4–10, where I am reminded of how I'm seated with Christ in heavenly places. Then I tell the devil, "I'm above you, and you are defeated in Jesus's name."

We have to believe what the Word of God says. Every day, enemies are opposing our faith and seeking to lead us to unbelief. In the fight for faith, we have to make sure all unbelief in God is quenched. By reading and meditating on the Word of God, we exercise faith in what the Lord has told us. This, in turn, strengthens our faith.

When Paul told Timothy to *"fight the good fight of faith,"* bad things were happening in the church. Many people were being led astray by lust and temptations, with some even becoming discouraged and losing their faith.

Our enemy doesn't appear with red horns and a pitchfork; Satan is a liar and a sneak. If allowed, he slips in the back door and then plants all kinds of negative thoughts, so we lose the awe of God we once had. To fight the good fight of faith requires us to abide in the Word by faith, regardless of what we feel or what we think we understand. Instead, we stand resolutely fastened in the Word in the power of the Spirit of God.

STAND BY HIS WORD

When I moved to California, not knowing what my next step would be, I began to strengthen myself by reading the Word. If I had allowed discouragement to subtly enter my heart, I would have packed my bags, moved back home, and started traveling again with my grandmother. Life in California was dramatically different than life ministering on the road. To be honest, there were times that I thought about my old life and how fulfilling and financially freeing it was.

I trusted God, but sometimes, it was a struggle. Once, I got a phone call from my sister Hannah, who had taken my place and was traveling with my grandmother as her assistant. She said, "Branden, we are flying to Australia and then Hawaii." Yes, there were meetings, but there was also some time for vacationing. I was happy for Hannah, but even though I was in sunny California, I didn't have much money and I was living in a small trailer. The heat would overpower the air conditioner on a regular basis.

But I had made a decision requiring courage and knowledge. I was following the divine plan for my life, so when discouragement slipped in, I stood on the words I was reading in the Bible. I held them to be true, and it defeated the enemy's attempts to eliminate me.

To resist the enemy, you must have courage; without it, the enemy will beat you every time. Courage is not a miracle; it comes by spending time in the Bible and proclaiming it over your life, even praying for courage! Here is a simple prayer that

I pray often: "Lord, I pray You to give me courage as Your Word says in Proverbs 28:1, '*The wicked flee when no one pursues, but the righteous are bold as a lion.*'"

In all things that confront you, be strong in the Lord and the strength of His might.

The year 2020 brought considerable challenges that started with the pandemic, leading to canceled meetings and our income taking a hit. I felt the pressure but resisted the enemy, refusing to surrender. I told Destanie that God would supply all our needs *"according to His riches in glory by Christ Jesus"* (Philippians 4:19). That became a continuous proclamation, declaring the Word of God over the situation.

Brother Kenneth E. Hagin said that blessings don't fall on us like ripe cherries falling off a tree. You have to work the Word. You see what the Word says, believe it in your heart, and proclaim it. Hagin also said that if you stand by the Word, God will stand by you and will make His Word good in your life.

I didn't sit there worrying or being sad. I knew what the Bible said, and I believed it and proclaimed it over us and our ministry. The Bible doesn't state, "My God shall supply all your needs according to you preaching only at churches." No! Thank God for that. My provider is Jesus—and He's your provider, too. The Lord may use your job to provide for you and your family, but *He* is your provider, and we should never get the two mixed up.

TAKE CHANCES AND TRUST GOD

The poetic words of Amy Carmichael ring like a bell, calling us to say "yes" to the Lord:

Strength of my heart, I need not fail—
Not mine to fear but to obey,
With such a leader who could quail?
Thou art as Thou wert yesterday!
Strength of my heart, I rest in Thee;
Fulfill Thy purposes through me.[7]

WE DON'T CONTROL WHEN GOD ANSWERS, BUT WE CAN CONTROL HOW WE TRUST HIM, KNOWING HE WILL CONTRIBUTE WHAT WE NEED, OFTEN IN ABUNDANCE.

We don't control when God answers, but we can control how we trust Him, knowing He will contribute what we need, often in abundance. By proclaiming God's Word over us, I positioned myself to be blessed by God—and it happened. God supernaturally supported us and provided for us in a way we had never seen before. From that moment, our ministry surged in growth in every category. During those days, the Lord dropped thoughts in my spirit about hosting a prayer meeting twice a month, focused on praying for California and America, believing for a mighty move of God to sweep across the whole country as never before.

We decided to take a risk, branch out, and host those prayer meetings, which we are still doing consistently twice a month.

7. Amy Carmichael, *Mountain Breezes: The Collected Poems of Amy Carmichael* (Fort Washington, PA: CLC Publications, 2013).

The decision took courage and faith in God. I didn't see the fruit immediately, but that's how faith works. At our first prayer meeting, thousands of people watched online and prayed with us. If you choose to fight, you must have courage.

Having courage keeps you trusting God, even when the situation seems impossible. There are times when you cannot afford another day of depression and discouragement; your faith, family, and friends need you to be courageous at all times!

When I ask people to tell me their definition of courage, I hear many different responses, but the one that I love the best is, "Courage is trust in God."

The most extraordinary people in the Bible were great because they trusted God and His plan for their lives. Even when some of them missed the mark, they found the courage to dare to repent and trust God would take care of them. The devil loves to poke fun at people and discourage them by lying and telling them they are not good enough, or they messed up and it's too late. That's why it's so vital to hear what God says about you personally and in the Word and quickly put your faith in God that you will always have courage.

Jonah is a perfect example of someone whose failure was not final. God gave Jonah the prophet a golden opportunity to go to Nineveh to give those people a chance to repent from their wickedness. But there was one problem: the reluctant prophet didn't want to go! He had heard how repulsive and corrupt Nineveh was and probably didn't have the courage to go there anyhow. So, Jonah deviated from God's plan and headed to Tarshish, seeking to flee from God's presence and get far away from Nineveh—almost two thousand and five hundred miles away! (See Jonah 1:3.)

We all know what happened next in that infamous story. While Jonah was on the ship to Tarshish, a storm was brewing, and sailors thought Jonah was the bad omen causing it, so they cast him into the sea. Miraculously, a whale swallowed Jonah, saving his life, at least for the moment. (See Jonah 1:17.)

Jonah learned a critical lesson. You can't run from God! Trapped in the belly of a whale, Jonah recognized his mistake and repented. If he lacked the courage to do so, he might still be in the whale's belly to this day! Though he, in his failure, could have been consumed by guilt, he chose to worship God and asked for forgiveness. Jonah finished the prophet's task, went to Nineveh, preached the gospel, and the people repented. Nineveh was spared.

Worshipping God is not based on how you feel but based on who He is. Courage is a sign of trusting God and a way of worshipping Him.

THE GREATNESS OF GOD

William Faulkner said, "You cannot swim for new horizons until you have courage to lose sight of the shore."

Jesus exemplified the wonder of courage when He mysteriously walked on water and performed other miracles. And Peter demonstrated similar courage when he got out of the boat and walked on water toward Jesus, even if it was just for a little bit.

After Jesus's death, resurrection, and ascension, having been with Him throughout His ministry, John wrote, *"He who is in you is greater than he who is in the world"* (1 John 4:4). The greater

One lives on inside us and is the source of our courage to get out of the boat.

PEOPLE OF FAITH SEE THE GLORIOUS FUTURE GOD HAS IN STORE FOR THEM INSTEAD OF CHAOS AND CALAMITY.

People of faith see the glorious future God has in store for them instead of chaos and calamity. There was a time when I didn't have the courage or dare to say "yes" to the call of God on my life. I tried everything else in different occupations, all the while knowing God had other plans for me. To grow, I had to get on the right path with God, and I eventually said "yes" to His calling.

> *We have become his poetry, a re-created people that will fulfill the destiny he has given each of us, for we are joined to Jesus, the Anointed One. Even before we were born, God planned in advance our destiny and the good works we would do to fulfill it!* (Ephesians 2:10 TPT)

In God's eternal counsels and by the declarations of His Word, we are destined for God's will to be fulfilled for each of us. He had a specially designed plan for you before you were born. Our God is a master-planner, and His plan is designed to give you the very best life. He pays attention to the smallest details of creation, details unimaginable and incomprehensible, from the beauty of each flower to the incredible depths of the ocean. *"He gave the sea its boundary so the waters would not over-step his command"* (Proverbs 8:29 NIV). If the Father pays close attention to every created thing, then rest assured that He has a unique, detailed, and blessed plan for your life.

When I decided to get back on track and say yes to God's calling, I devoted myself to spending more time in His presence and reading the Word. The greater my commitment, the deeper my hunger for God increased. I didn't even recognize the man I had become! This is key: if you want to make a genuine change in your life, you must give God's Word first place in it.

The famous writer and pastor Andrew Murray said that daily fellowship with God is the source of power. To be a man of God of this spiritual caliber requires spending time with Him. Fellowship with God jump-started my life, leading to significant changes evident to all who knew me. One fateful night, it came to a head at a meeting where I received a special touch from God. This encounter further amplified what God was doing in my life.

One night, while worshipping God, I suddenly felt a great sense of freedom from all the things distracting me and taking away my time with God. When the change happened, I rear-ranged my schedule to spend time with Him. Back then, girls had been a prominent disruption. As I continued to spend time with God, I heard Him say that I would have a special girl in my life soon, but she would be different. She would help me build my relationship with God.

If you're a single person who is seeking the right husband or wife, look for someone who will add to you and help you strengthen your relationship with God, not make it weaker. Marriage is about a union of beliefs and doing things together like joining your faith with each other, sowing money together, going to church and serving together, and praying with each other. God should be the number one priority for both of you. You don't want to be with someone who challenges your walk with God or discourages you. God designed us to have a help-mate, not a burden-mate. I was in wrong relationships with girls who were a burden. Your partner needs to add to you as a person.

Fortunately, when I met Destanie, we made the right choice.

Before we met, I was already studying what it meant to be a person of courage. I was so fired up about the subject that I told my grandmother that, if she ever wanted me to speak on her radio show, all I could talk about was courage. Often, what becomes a passion will eventually be your life. Little did I know that the courage I was learning wasn't to teach others but was instead for myself.

POWER IN THE NAME OF JESUS

In Acts 2:16–17, Peter used the prophetic words of Joel and declared:

> But this is what was spoken by the prophet Joel: "And it shall come to pass in the last days, says God, that I will pour out of My Spirit on all flesh; your sons and your daughters shall prophesy, your **young men shall see visions**, and your old men shall dream dreams."

I was reading my Bible, and the words *"young men shall see visions"* struck me like lightning because I had a vision of heaven in which I attended a class on courage taught by King David. I will share it with you in a later chapter. Please understand, even writing this book has required a lot of courage for a young man like me. But I trusted the Lord and began to write.

Over the years, I have had quite a few men of God prophesy about me writing a book, but I gave that desire to God, knowing He would tell me the right time to start writing. Even when I first met Destanie's dad, Rick Reyna, the first thing he said to me was, "God is calling you to write a book!" Finally, I dared to start writing. Courage isn't just something you master; it's a lifetime experience because walking by faith requires different levels of courage.

COURAGE ISN'T JUST SOMETHING YOU MASTER; IT'S A LIFETIME EXPERIENCE BECAUSE WALKING BY FAITH REQUIRES DIFFERENT LEVELS OF COURAGE.

Anytime I ever feel discouraged, I take time to be alone in my prayer closet. Inside that quiet place, I have a chair, and all of my faith-filled books are piled next to it. I sit there and begin to read the Word and worship God. By the time I emerge from that sweet place of God's presence, I'm ready to go. Any discouragement has disappeared because God has given us authority over any negativity from the enemy.

Our ministry was born in a small trailer, which became the secret place of prayer and revelation. In those days, I received a message about the power in the name of Jesus. I cried out to God early one morning, sensing that He called me to preach, but I didn't even have a message to preach. I told Him this out loud and also proclaimed that I don't like to even talk to people. That's when I heard God say, "I'll give you the message, and I'll preach it through you."

The first message I preached was entitled "The Power in the Name of Jesus," based on Acts 3:16. After Peter healed the lame man, he declared:

> And His name, through **faith in His name**, has made this man strong, whom you see and know. Yes, the faith which comes through Him has given him this perfect soundness in the presence of you all.

Believing in the power that is in the name of Jesus is what healed the lame man. Jesus's name is the most powerful name on earth. Don't ever say you haven't been given anything, for you have received the name that's above every name. (See Philippians 2:9.) Supernatural signs follow that name; demons are cast out, and the sick are made whole. That's the authority that belongs to the name of Jesus. Hell shakes when it hears the name of Jesus, with demons trembling at its very utterance!

We named our ministry His Name Ministries based on Acts 3:16. We have now traveled the world preaching that message.

A SUPERNATURAL EXPERIENCE

The supernatural experience I referred to earlier happened when I was around fourteen years old. As I was sleeping, Jesus visited me in a dream or night vision. Before this encounter, I wasn't spending much time at all with God. I used to attend a Christian school, where we would have Bible class each morning.

But it wasn't long before I switched to a public school and was suddenly surrounded by bad influences, cut off from the healthy environment to which I was accustomed.

The move weighed heavily on me. I stopped spending time with God and His Word altogether. But seeing Jesus changed everything! In my dream, Jesus said to me, "Branden, why have you forsaken Me? Why haven't you been spending time with Me?"

To hear those words was like a supernatural download in my spirit. *Wow,* I thought, *Jesus knows I haven't been reading the Bible or praying, and He wants me to spend time with Him!*

The God of the universe also wants *you* to spend time with Him! Even now, He longs for you to fellowship with Him. No one prays to God like you. No one worships God like you. We each fellowship with God in a unique way that is special to Him.

It hurt when Jesus asked me why I had forsaken Him. The word "forsaken" means to turn your back on someone with whom you once had fellowship. In Psalm 22:1, David uses the word as he prophesies about Jesus on the cross, when Jesus cried out, *"My God, my God, why have You forsaken Me?"* (Matthew 27:46). At that moment, God had to turn His back on His only Son. As the prophet Isaiah said:

> *It's what GOD had in mind all along, to crush him with pain. The plan was that he give himself as an offering for sin so that he'd see life come from it—life, life, and more life. And GOD's plan will deeply prosper through him.*
>
> (Isaiah 53:10 MSG)

In my dream, I began to cry out, "I'm sorry, Lord! I'm so sorry!" He looked at me, with eyes full of love and compassion, and replied, "It's okay. I forgive you."

What stuck with me the most in this encounter was the way He looked upon me. There was a smile on His face, and His eyes were full of so much love that my body couldn't even comprehend it. I began to feel myself crumble, almost falling down; I couldn't even look at Him. All I could do was say, "Sorry!" over and over again. Jesus then looked upon me with His fiery eyes of love and spoke softly and beautifully, "It's okay, Branden."

I finally looked up and saw that I was in the air with Him. I watched as we flew over streets full of people who were almost frozen while trying to warm themselves by the meager fires they created. The air was so cold in the vision that I could feel the goosebumps rising all over my arms.

After we watched them for a while, Jesus said to me, "It's not my fault they're in this situation; I've done everything I could for them. These people are hurting. Help them and heal them." After He finished speaking, I woke up back in my bedroom. The dream had ended.

The next day, I told my family everything that happened in my dream, and they responded with their theories about what it meant. I appreciated their words, but I knew what they said wasn't what Jesus was trying to tell me.

Years passed before I understood the whole meaning of the dream. One day, while living in that same small trailer in California, a flash of remembrance came to me. As I thought about how much that one vision had changed my life, I heard a voice inside of me say, "Do you want to know what it means?" I responded with an enthusiastic, "Yes!"

I heard the Lord ask, "What is it that you preach?"

I said, "I speak about the power that's in the name of Jesus."

He said, "Everything I did for humanity is in My name, and when you go and preach My name, I will help them and heal them."

ANYTHING YOU NEED IS IN HIS NAME! ARE YOU HURTING? DO YOU NEED A TOUCH FROM HIM? IT'S ALL IN THE MIGHTY NAME OF JESUS!

Wow, what a word! And Jesus is saying the same to you: anything you need is in His name! Are you hurting? Do you need a touch from Him? It's all in the mighty name of Jesus! Take courage, for it is finished through the name of Jesus. Take courage, for your prayers are answered through His name. Sickness can't touch your house because of His name. Poverty can't stay in the name of Jesus. Jesus tells us that He has already done everything required for victory—it's all in His name!

Encourage yourself in the knowledge that He won the victory for us two thousand years ago. I believe that by the time you're done reading this book, you're going to be living a courageous life like never before.

3

FINDING COURAGE

It is the living Word on your lips that heals sick folks,
that saves lost men, that puts courage and strength
into the faint-hearted.
—*E. W. Kenyon*

The phrase "Do not fear" or something similar is the most repeated commandment in the Bible, said more than two hundred times. The verses on fear are often connected with courage. For example:

> *Be strong and of good courage, **do not fear** nor be afraid of them; for the LORD your God, He is the One who goes with you. He will not leave you nor forsake you.*
>
> (Deuteronomy 31:6)

It is one thing to say, "Don't be afraid." But threats are a powerful force that can seize us and render us powerless to act. That is why the second half of this verse is so important, for it gives us the motive and power to be strong and courageous. Moses assured the people that the Lord would go with them and they would win the battle against the Amalekites. (See Exodus 17:8–13.) Imagine the courage that comes when you enter battle with the mighty, most powerful God of Israel standing by your side!

Courage is not a gift; it is an act only needed in times of danger. Eleanor Roosevelt once said, "You have to accept whatever comes, and the only important thing is that you meet it with courage and with the best that you have to give."

God makes the difference.

On February 26, 1955, North American Aviation test pilot George Smith realized something was wrong with the new F-100 jet he was flying. The controls would not budge, and he was diving straight toward the Pacific Ocean at more than seven hundred miles per hour—faster than the speed of sound! He had to eject and hope for the best.

Smith survived, but his injuries were horrendous, and he was initially afraid to ever fly again. But he remembered the encouraging words of the schoolchildren who wrote to him, having heard the jet's sonic boom. "You are a very brave man to bale out of that aeroplane...I hope you will still be a test pilot," one wrote. Another said, "I would like to be as heroic as you."[8]

Nelson Mandela faced his fears with courage, overcoming persecution and imprisonment to become the president of South Africa. Mandela said, "I learned that courage was not the absence of fear, but the triumph over it. I felt fear myself more times than I can remember, but I hid it behind a mask of

8. William Coughlin, "Courage Is Not a Sometime Thing," *Reader's Digest*, February 1956; archive.org/details/dli.bengal.10689.11994/page/n195/mode/2up.

boldness. The brave man is not he who does not feel afraid, but he who conquers that fear."[9]

NELSON MANDELA SAID, "THE BRAVE MAN IS NOT HE WHO DOES NOT FEEL AFRAID, BUT HE WHO CONQUERS THAT FEAR."

Upon his liberation, Mandela took opportunities to speak at significant Christian events, including the Zionist Christian Church's Easter conferences in 1992 and 1994. During the latter, he shared this message:

> The Good News [was] borne by our risen Messiah who chose not one race, who chose not one country, who chose not one language, who chose not one tribe, who chose all of humankind!…Each Easter marks the rebirth of our faith. It marks the victory of our risen Saviour over the torture of the cross and the grave. Our Messiah, who came to us in the form of a mortal man, but who by his suffering and crucifixion attained immortality.[10]

BE COURAGEOUS

Whether we jump out of a jet, are imprisoned, or take risk by following God to unknown places, it requires courage to win over fear.

9. Nelson Mandela, *Long Walk to Freedom* (Boston: Back Bay Books, 1995).
10. "Speech by Nelson Mandela at Zionist Christian Church Easter Conference Moria, 3 April 1994," South African History Online; www.sahistory.org.za/archive/speech-nelson-mandela-zionist-christian-church-easter-conference-moria-3-april-1994.

We may not think we are capable of courage, but God commands us to be courageous just the same. God's presence strengthens and encourages us to make the right decision and do what is right. The Scriptures indicate that we should be courageous by an act of the will, but God's empowering presence enflames our courage.

Paul told the Ephesian church, *"Be strong in the Lord and in the power of His might"* (Ephesians 6:10). In similar language, Paul told the Corinthian church, *"Watch, stand fast in the faith, be brave, be strong"* (1 Corinthians 16:13).

Consider this verse in the book of Acts, in which the Lord tells the apostle Paul to take courage when he goes into a dangerous place in Jerusalem, followed by an involuntary journey to Rome:

> *The following night the Lord stood near Paul and said, "Take courage! As you have testified about me in Jerusalem, so you must also testify in Rome."* (Acts 23:11 NIV)

There is little doubt that Paul was a man of courage. His message concerning Christ plus his commitment to opening the doors to the gentiles made him the subject of threats, torture, and imprisonment. On this occasion, his words led to a scuffle; while some Jews took his side, Paul learned that a team of forty assassins took oaths to kill him. Jesus knew that Paul would need even greater courage on his next leg of the journey, so He appeared to encourage Paul to *take* the trip despite the danger.

COURAGE, WILL, AND ACTION

Courage requires activating our will. And, for the followers of Jesus, it's not just our raw willpower that instills courage, but the will collaborating in faith with God's purposes and plans.

In Philippians 2:13, Paul clarifies that God nudges our will to respond positively to our decisions according to God's will, "*for it is God who works in you both to will and to do for His good pleasure.*" As we turn our will to Him, God empowers us and supports us every step of the way.

> *Christ Jesus, who, being in the form of God, did not consider it robbery to be equal with God, but made Himself of no reputation, taking the form of a bondservant, and coming in the likeness of men.* (Philippians 2:5–7)

Jesus wasn't a servant; He chose to serve, humbling Himself and becoming a man so we could become like Him, breaking Adam's curse. Jesus said, "*I have come down from heaven, not to do My own will, but the will of Him who sent Me*" (John 6:38). As He chose to do the will of His Father, so should we.

Jesus defeated death, hell, sickness, disease, and poverty, made us alive with Him, and then raised us up to sit together in heavenly places. God, "*even when we were dead in trespasses, made us alive together with Christ (by grace you have been saved), and raised us up together, and made us sit together in the heavenly places in Christ Jesus*" (Ephesians 2:5–6). Our position, seated in heavenly places in Christ Jesus, gives us courage so we can overcome by God's power.

COURAGE MOTIVATED BY HIS LOVING MERCY

One morning, I heard the audible voice of God saying, "My mercies are new every morning." What a merciful God we serve! The psalmist declared, "*The LORD is gracious and full of compassion, slow to anger and great in mercy*" (Psalm 145:8). The Hebrew word for "mercy" is *chêsêd*, meaning "loving-kindness," "affection," and "associated with favor and grace." Because of mercy, we have the courage to obey His will and stand firm in dangerous situations.

God's mercy is manifest in His great love for us. (See Ephesians 2:4). Jesus was motivated by love to courageously face the Jews and Romans, suffering torture and dying a cruel death on a cross. Love provokes courage and mercy, and so will you when the opportunity appears to demonstrate your love with courageous acts. *"Greater love has no one than this, than to lay down one's life for his friends"* (John 15:13). With those words, Jesus foreshadowed His own death, but He also told us that the utmost form of love is the courage to stand resolved for another. Love of God and love of neighbor equals bravery when needed.

When I was younger, I kept telling God how much I loved Him one night as I was lying in bed. After I fell asleep, I heard these words: "Look up how much I love you." Indeed, God demonstrated His love for us in these oft-quoted words from the Gospel of John: *"For God so loved the world that He gave His only begotten Son"* (John 3:16). Heaven presented its best for us not with words only but also in action when Jesus came and walked among us. *This is love.* Jesus said, *"As the Father loved Me, I also have loved you; abide in My love"* (John 15:9). I don't know about you, but this encourages me and gives me courage!

I experienced a tough time in a prayer movement in San Francisco. It was one of those times in life where you can't see where you were going and just exist by putting one foot in front of the other. There's a mystery surrounding you, and you don't know what's coming. You can't go back, and you just have to trust.

God is not abandoning us in those places of waiting. He's with us on our whole journey. When we get to the end of our process, we can look back and see that He's been with us every step of the way. He lights up the road ahead of us and the road behind us.

BOLD AS A LION

The wicked flee when no one pursues, but the righteous are **bold as a lion.** (Proverbs 28:1)

The wicked take refuge in flight because their despicable, corrupt consciences make them cowards. Something about being depraved and malicious leads to fear. But a pure heart gives a person courage. Being virtuous leads to boldness.

As Christians, we do not surrender to fear, but we live by faith and courage because perfect love casts out all fear. God chases cowards broken by sin to transform their hearts, calling them to live a life of courage—to be bold as a lion.

Night and day, Martin Luther, the Catholic monk, pondered the book of Romans until he found the link between God's justice and the earth-shattering statement, *"The just shall live by faith"* (Romans 1:17). In a moment of divine inspiration, Luther grasped that the justice of God is righteousness through grace and sheer mercy from God, justifying us through faith. The Scriptures came alive, and his heart burned. His life was one long act of lionhearted boldness against the abuses of the Roman church and for the glory of the gospel. The insignificant monk stood against the Catholic empire that was against him. When we get radically free from fear, then the righteous can be as bold as a lion for the sake of the gospel!

The lion is the king of the jungle because it has no fear. Instead, the other animals fear the lion. It's the king of beasts, the monarch of the forest, and an emblem of kingly authority and power. Although John the Baptist called Jesus *"the Lamb of God who takes away the sin of the world"* (John 1:29), Jesus is also the Lion of Judah. Jesus was the sacrificial lamb who opened the door for salvation for all, but He is a mighty King.

AS CHRISTIANS, WE DO NOT SURRENDER TO FEAR, BUT WE LIVE BY FAITH AND COURAGE BECAUSE PERFECT LOVE CASTS OUT ALL FEAR.

In the book of Revelation, the apostle John wrote:

One of the elders said to me, "Do not weep. Behold, the Lion of the tribe of Judah, the Root of David."
(Revelation 5:5)

The lion was the ancient symbol of the tribe of Judah. Jacob described his son Judah as *"a lion's whelp"* (Genesis 49:9). According to tradition, the standard of Judah in Israel's encampment was a lion, the symbol of strength, courage, and sovereignty.

"The righteous are bold as a lion" (Proverbs 28:1). I have always stood on those words. Even when I had opportunities to quit or be discouraged and even scared, I would tell myself over and over, "I'm bold as a lion because I'm the righteousness of God!" Meditating on Scriptures is invaluable for implanting the truth in your mind and heart. As you meditate on this verse, you build faith, and you will have courage as you have never

experienced before. Even when a challenging situation arises, you will sense courage. You will *"be strong in the Lord and in the power of His might"* (Ephesians 6:10). You will experience bold-as-a-lion courage.

MEDITATING ON SCRIPTURES IS INVALUABLE FOR IMPLANTING THE TRUTH IN YOUR MIND AND HEART.

When Jesus walked the earth, He dared to stand against those who opposed Him with no timidity. Yes, He was the Lion of the tribe of Judah, even at the age of twelve.

Heading home to Nazareth after spending the Passover in Jerusalem, Mary and Joseph realized Jesus was not among the group of travelers, so they returned to the city. After three days of frantic searching:

> *They found Him in the temple, sitting in the midst of the teachers, both listening to them and asking them questions. And all who heard Him were astonished at His understanding and answers.* (Luke 2:46–47)

Even at that young age, Jesus dared to remain in the temple, talking with such learned men and not even concerned about being alone without his parents. When His mother and His foster father finally found him, they were probably crying tears of both joy and frustration.

And He said to them, "Why did you seek Me? Did you not know that I must be about My Father's business?"

(Luke 2:49)

FEARLESS JESUS

By example, Jesus demonstrated how to live life at a courageous level without fear. Jesus confronted wild and crazy demon-possessed people and cast out the demons. Most people would run away, but not Jesus. He stood His ground and healed them all because of His love for people.

Jesus walked with such authority and courage during His ministry. Without fear, He bravely exposed the religious leaders who were misleading people with false teachings. He continued to preach despite opposition from His religious opponents, and twice, without fear, He boldly cleansed the temple, driving out those who were defiling worship. (See John 2:13–16; Matthew 21:12–13.)

In Mark 16:15, Jesus gathered the disciples and gave them the Great Commission: *"Go into all the world and preach the gospel to every creature."* Like Jesus, they would go into dangerous territory while spreading the gospel everywhere. Jesus didn't tell a select few to stand on platforms with microphones to preach the gospel; He wanted everyone to share the good news of Christ and His kingdom.

Jesus didn't send His disciples out without a weapon to use, but followed up with a word that they would have power over all their enemies in His name. The weapon they would use daily is powerful in the Holy Spirit. Jesus assured them:

*And these signs will follow those who believe: **In My name**
they will cast out demons; they will speak with new tongues;
they will take up serpents; and if they drink anything deadly,
it will by no means hurt them; they will lay hands on the
sick, and they will recover.* (Mark 16:17–18)

Their enemies were subject to them. As Jesus gave them the
power to overcome, He gave us the power to be courageous in
our times.

Sometimes, we don't see what the enemy sees because we
walk in the light of Christ, who is the light of the world. Isaiah 2:5
says, "*Come and let us walk in the light of the* LORD." At other times,
the light God gives us exposes the work of the enemy. We have
experienced this several times while traveling in our ministry.

A STORY WITH A BOLD ENDING

One night, Destanie and I were out of town on a ministry
trip and had spent some time with friends. We were going to
leave very early the following morning, so we decided to fill up
the gas tank on the rental car. As I was pumping gas, Destanie
remained inside the car. I was talking to the Lord under my
breath when I heard a noise. I didn't think anything of it until I
heard in my spirit, "Branden, he is going to try to rob you."

That's not a message you want to hear! I wanted to hear
God say that I am His good and faithful servant, or "My son, a
great reward is coming your way." As I looked around, I saw a
guy approaching me fast, hiding something in his pocket. There
was a car parked right behind him. My mind began to race as I
thought, *What can I do?!* I couldn't run away because Destanie
was in the car.

Quickly, the promises of the Bible come to me: in My name, you have authority. I told myself, "I'm going to use the name!" But then I wondered, *How do I do that?* The answer came quickly to my spirit: "Say it! Speak it!"

So I shouted at my would-be robber, "Jesus loves you and has a plan for your life!"

Screaming very loudly, he responded, "I see it! I see it! It's all over you."

Spreading the gospel and being courageous isn't something you just talk about—you walk in it! Talk the talk and walk the walk.

My words for the man started to flow like a mighty river as the presence of God was thick at the gas station. When I was done speaking, I prayed for him, and the situation changed from an attempted robbery to a God moment, a mountaintop experience. Everything was confirmed by the word spoken in His name, and no enemy could touch me.

As I got into the car, Destanie asked, "Was he going to rob you?" She told me that she had seen four other people hiding near the parked car, and its engine was running. She told me it looked like they were waiting to see if he could rob me—but God moved instead!

Courage is there when you must stand against anything the enemy may try to throw against you. I couldn't even sleep that night, but as I was praying, I heard the Lord saying, "Branden, I'll never leave you nor forsake you!"

Take courage! God will never leave you nor forsake *you* either. Stop believing the enemy's lies. The Lord says, "I will never fail you, and I will never abandon you." (See Deuteronomy 31:6.) We can say with confidence:

> *For He Himself has said, "I will never leave you nor forsake you." So we may boldly say: "The LORD is my helper; I will not fear. What can man do to me?"* (Hebrews 13:5–6)

Say it with confidence and know that it is true!

**STOP BELIEVING THE ENEMY'S LIES.
THE LORD SAYS, "I WILL NEVER FAIL YOU,
AND I WILL NEVER ABANDON YOU."**

WE ARE THE RIGHTEOUSNESS OF GOD

We are the righteousness of God because of what Jesus did for us. The word "righteous" means "in right standing with God." Those who accept Jesus as their Savior become the righteousness of God. It is not something we deserved; it was freely given to us through Christ.

> *For if, by the trespass of the one man, death reigned through that one man, how much more will those who receive God's abundant provision of grace and of the gift of righteousness **reign** in life through the one man, Jesus Christ!*
> (Romans 5:17 NIV)

We reign with Jesus in life. The Greek word for "reign" is *basileus*, which means "king," "sovereign," "leader," or "ruler."

So, we are kings in this life now and will reign with Christ in heaven! It is life by the righteousness of God. We reign not as victims but as victors through what Jesus did.

Romans 5:19 says, "*For as by one man's disobedience many were made sinners, so also by one Man's obedience many will be made righteous.*" The many made righteous includes you and me! Through Jesus's obedience, many are transformed from unholy living to a life of righteousness, resulting in the boldness of a lion.

Righteousness is not associated with keeping the law or how much you pray and spend time with God, even though we are called to live this way. We can't rest our faith on our own abilities or accomplishments. We don't brag about what we have done but honor what Christ did on an old rugged cross, where the power of sin was broken and we were made righteous by His blood. God wants us to live a life worthy of His works for us, not put our trust in all the wrong places.

I learned this personally. Being in full-time ministry, I spend a lot of time in prayer and reading the Word. One day, I realized I was putting my faith in the fact that I was praying more than most people. God corrected me. He told me, "It's not your righteousness, Branden, but Christ's righteousness, so put your faith in that."

I had been putting my faith in my daily schedule of prayer and reading God's Word rather than in what Jesus had done to make me the righteousness of God. To live a courageous and bold life, you must understand everything Jesus did for you. He has made you the righteousness of God, so reign in life now. Have courage! Be bold as a lion.

4

HOW I BEGAN TO STUDY COURAGE

Our praying needs to be pressed and pursued with an
energy that never tires, a persistency which will not be
denied, and a courage that never fails.
—*E. M. Bounds*

You cannot discover how courageous you are until you are willing to find out how far you can go in life.

I was in a serious season of spending time in the Word, asking the Holy Spirit to show me what to read and what the Spirit was saying to me. It seemed like I was constantly guided toward one subject: the theme of courage. I was almost consumed with the word "courage," biblical examples of courage, and how necessary God considers courage to be.

When David took on the Philistines' champion, Goliath, it appeared that the men of Israel lacked the courage to face him because, at that moment, the men lacked faith. (See 1 Samuel 17:22–50.)

Faith was being built in my life when I began to study courage. *"Faith comes by hearing, and hearing by the word of God"* (Romans 10:17). The repetition of hearing the Word results in greater faith. Faith was coming; I could see the results in my life, and I could sense the godly courage.

In Jude 1:20, the author wrote these compelling words: *"But you, beloved, building yourselves up on your most holy faith, praying in the Holy Spirit."* Your faith is the foundation that supports your soul, including your thinking, willingness, and actions. Faith is the seedbed of courage, and I was planting seeds.

As I mentioned earlier, I told my grandmother, Dr. Billye Brim, that I could share what I learned about courage from God's Word if she needed a speaker on her radio show. I would never have had the boldness to say something like that, except I was so consumed by studying courage, it seemed like everywhere I looked in the Bible, courage was there. Little did I know that courage wasn't for the radio listeners; courage was for me!

I needed godly courage more than anyone I knew. I was fighting against the call of God on my life. I always sensed God's presence tugging at my heart, yet I would ignore it. Once I began to study courage in the Bible, I kept finding it, begging for my attention. God never left me; He was always there, and He just wanted me to say "yes" to His plan for my life, which took courage.

To do what God calls you to do takes courage and boldness while trusting God at all times, no matter what. Never listen to what your mind or emotions may say. Don't lean on your own understanding. These words from Proverbs made an impact on me: *"Every word of God is pure; He is a shield to those who put their trust in Him"* (Proverbs 30:5). God's pure words can be tested and proved in the furnace of experience, and He defends those who put their trust in Him. I don't know about you, but it gives me courage to know that I can trust God because He is my shield no matter the circumstances. Even writing this book is an act of obedience and faith.

GOD'S PURE WORDS CAN BE TESTED AND PROVED IN THE FURNACE OF EXPERIENCE, AND HE DEFENDS THOSE WHO PUT THEIR TRUST IN HIM.

TWELVE SPIES IN THE FACE OF DANGER

Israel endured years of slavery in Egypt, but was delivered into freedom by the great I Am. They saw miracles in the desert, water gushing from rocks, clouds by day for shade and a cloud on fire by night, and a supernatural provision in the middle of the desert. God took care of them with the miracles of bread and water, the tent of meeting, and Moses on the mountain of God, receiving the Ten Commandments.

Though Israel was accustomed to wandering in the desert for months, it would be impossible for two million people to trek continuously across the barren sand. Most of the time, they were concerned about food, water, and occasional enemies as they moved from one oasis to the next. Finally, they arrived at Kadesh Barnea, close to the promised land.

In Numbers 13, God tells Moses to send out a dozen undercover agents to discover the needed information about their enemies' cities, fortifications, and armies. One would think they would be resilient, ready, and eager to settle down. This was the promised land, flowing with milk and honey and filled with every fruit imaginable. (See Numbers 13:27.) But ten spies focused on the giants living there. They reported:

> The land through which we have gone as spies is a land that devours its inhabitants, and all the people whom we saw in it are men of great stature. There we saw the giants (the descendants of Anak came from the giants); and we were like grasshoppers in our own sight, and so we were in their sight. (Numbers 13:32–33)

So despite the fact that the land of Canaan was everything that God had promised, they focused on the fortified cities and the size of their opponents.

The consequences are disastrous when we don't believe in God's promises. A whole generation did not enter the land of promise because the people were afraid to trust God.

> Now with whom was He angry forty years? Was it not with those who sinned, whose corpses fell in the wilderness? And to whom did He swear that they would not enter His rest, but to those who did not obey? So, we see that they could not enter in because of unbelief. (Hebrews 3:17–19)

Two spies, Joshua and Caleb, tried to counter the people's fatalistic attitude by reassuring them. "Caleb quieted the people before Moses, and said, 'Let us go up at once and take possession, for we are well able to overcome it'" (Numbers 13:30). However, the other ten spies implanted such fear in the people that the Israelite community began to weep with remorse, crying, "If only we had died in the land of Egypt! Or if only we had died in this wilderness!" (Numbers 14:2).

Joshua and Caleb kept pleading with the people to have faith and not rebel against the Lord, but the people responded by threatening to stone them.

The Lord had brought the people to the promised land. It was a time for courage and trust in God, not cowardice and doubt, but Israel wanted to stay in a comfortable and safe place. Moses was tired of their murmuring, complaining, and lack of faith. Being a man of God, he interceded on their behalf when God was ready to judge them.

The Lord told Moses:

Except for Caleb the son of Jephunneh and Joshua the son of Nun, you shall by no means enter the land which I swore I would make you dwell in. But your little ones, whom you said would be victims, I will bring in, and they shall know the land which you have despised. But as for you, your carcasses shall fall in this wilderness. And your sons shall be shepherds in the wilderness forty years, and bear the brunt of your infidelity, until your carcasses are consumed in the wilderness. According to the number of the days in which you spied out the land, forty days, for each day you shall bear your guilt one year, namely forty years, and you shall know My rejection. (Numbers 14:30–34)

Caleb and Joshua had spirits of courage and faith and eventually experienced God's best.

HAVE THE FAITH OF GOD

Jesus said, *"Have faith in God"* (Mark 11:22). According to Joseph Benson's *Commentary*, in the original Greek, this is, *"Have a faith of God"*—that is, God's full, perfect, effectual faith.

Like Peter walking on water, never lose your gaze or take your eyes off of Jesus, but trust Him at all times. If you focus in the wrong direction, down rather than up, you end up looking at the waves rather than the Lord. When Peter began to sink, Jesus said, *"O you of little faith, why did you doubt?"* (Matthew 14:31). Had Peter kept his eyes on Jesus, courage and faith would have prevailed.

I have learned that one of the keys to living a courageous life is to keep your eyes on Jesus, even when it seems to be impossible.

In Hebrews 12:1–2, entitled "the Race of Faith" in some Bible translations, the author encourages us to *"run with endurance the race that is set before us, **looking unto Jesus**, the author and finisher of our faith."* It's what Peter should have done. No matter what storm we face, or even what people are saying about us or the hurts of the past, we must take our eyes off our circumstances and look to Jesus!

Walking by faith is a courageous walk. Caleb and Joshua had the courage and faith to look at the situation differently than everybody else.

IF YOU FOCUS IN THE WRONG DIRECTION, DOWN RATHER THAN UP, YOU END UP LOOKING AT THE WAVES RATHER THAN THE LORD.

I'd like to share two more powerful examples of courage from the life of Joshua and Daniel and his friends, the three young Hebrew men.

JOSHUA, A MAN OF COURAGE

Have you ever wondered how Joshua and Caleb felt when they returned with the other ten spies after their expedition into Canaan? These two mighty men were the only ones out of the twelve spies to trust God. They were the only ones who believed God would give them victory though it seemed unsurmountable. But after forty years of wandering because of their disobedience, this motley band defeated the mighty armies that lived in Canaan mainly because of the strength and courage of Joshua.

Joshua was left in a vulnerable yet audacious place when he had to tell the people of Israel that Moses was dead and he would be the next leader who would guide them into Canaan, the land of the divine promise. Despite the challenge, Joshua found courage in God's words to him:

Every place that the sole of your foot will tread upon I have given you, as I said to Moses...No man shall be able to

stand before you all the days of your life; as I was with
Moses, so I will be with you. I will not leave you nor forsake
you.   (Joshua 1:3, 5)

God left some valuable instructions for Joshua, telling him
to *"be strong and of good courage,"* then doubling down by telling him to be *"very courageous"* (Joshua 1:6–7). Then God says
these final words for Joshua to consider and obey:

This Book of the Law shall not depart from your mouth,
but you shall meditate in it day and night, that you may
observe to do according to all that is written in it. For then
you will make your way prosperous, and then you will have
good success. Have I not commanded you? **Be strong and**
of good courage; *do not be afraid, nor be dismayed, for the*
LORD your God is with you wherever you go.
                                                    (Joshua 1:8–9)

God was telling Joshua to repeat His words frequently,
repeat them often, and speak of them to refresh his memory.
He was to meditate on them day and night, whenever he had
any leisure time away from the battle and serving the people.
(See also Psalm 1:2.) By doing these things, Joshua would be
a productive leader and have success, especially when battling
Israel's enemies.

Being surrounded by ungodliness, as Joshua was, is not easy,
but we can have courage everywhere we go as Christians. We
don't have to let darkness influence us one bit. Those of us living
in Los Angeles are surrounded by a very dark world. I have even
had ministers ask me how I do it.

I have heard stories of people being on fire for God and then moving to L.A. and becoming utterly lost and confused. When confronted with these stories, I tell them how important it is not to neglect your daily time with God, in His presence, and in the Word. The enemy will try to steal your time and extinguish your fire for God. I tell the ministers how I spend more time in prayer and the Word than I ever have before because I'm not ignorant of the devil's devices. I don't let the culture around me shift me; I move it!

We are the light of the world, so we take the light into the darkness, and our good works will glorify Christ. You are the temple of God. Be strong! Be brave wherever you go because God is always with you, just as God was with Moses and Joshua. He will be with you no matter what!

DANIEL AND HIS THREE FRIENDS

Daniel and his three Hebrew friends, Hananiah, Mishael, and Azariah, were taken from Jerusalem during a siege by King Nebuchadnezzar of Babylon. You might know the three Hebrews by their pagan names: Shadrach, Meshach, and Abed-Nego. Daniel's pagan name was Belteshazzar, which crops up at different times in the book of Daniel.

The four young men were captured to serve in the king's palace because they were *"good-looking, gifted in all wisdom, possessing knowledge and quick to understand"* (Daniel 1:4). They were probably from Judah's royal family or nobility. Most victorious kings in those ancient times would typically only allow their own people to rule and have influence; they would enslave all conquered peoples. But King Nebuchadnezzar resolved to train the best minds among the people within his kingdom, regardless of their origin.

Therefore, Daniel and his three friends were selected by the chief court official to be trained in the language and literature of the Babylonians, which allowed them to have some influence. Still, at the same time, they refused to participate in worshipping Babylon's idols or doing anything that would violate their faith in God. They had such courage and boldness in serving God! Talk about a tough situation. They were fully living in an ungodly culture.

Daniel and his Hebrew friends learned how to stand firm in a culture of compromise. Resistance is not futile; it is a sign of courage and faith in God. The king offered them royal rations and wine, the delicacies of rich foods fit for a king.

When surrounded by an ungodly culture and false gods, they had no choice but to follow the one true God, no matter what. *"Daniel purposed in his heart that he would not defile himself with the portion of the king's delicacies, nor with the wine which he drank"* (Daniel 1:8). It's likely that the food was unclean or defiled in one way or another; it may have been presented to the Babylonian gods before being served for meals. So, Daniel requested that the steward under the chief of the eunuchs allow them to eat a plant-based diet instead, which would have included vegetables, fruits, seeds, and legumes.

After ten days, it was apparent that Daniel and his friends looked healthier and much better than those who ate the king's delicacies. *"Thus the steward took away their portion of delicacies and the wine that they were to drink, and gave them vegetables"*

(Daniel 1:16). Not only that, but when the king brought Daniel and the three Hebrews before him, he discovered:

> *In all matters of wisdom and understanding about which the king examined them, he found them ten times better than all the magicians and astrologers who were in all his realm.* (Daniel 1:20)

Daniel, Shadrach, Meshach, and Abednego were courageous and trusted God to do the right thing in an adverse ungodly culture, so God gave them favor in the court of the king.

Every day, we too have opportunities to do the right thing and demonstrate moral courage. The world is dangerous for those who do evil and even for those who do nothing when the situation demands courage and faith in God.

THE WORLD IS DANGEROUS FOR THOSE WHO DO EVIL AND EVEN FOR THOSE WHO DO NOTHING WHEN THE SITUATION DEMANDS COURAGE AND FAITH IN GOD.

A NEW WAY OF THINKING

A man once approached me about a job he needed, but he explained that he had to pass a few tests before he could get it. The unfortunate part was that he told me he wasn't that smart or studious. I told him how important it was to change how he talked; he needed to speak more positively about himself.

Then, I shared with him the story in the Bible about Daniel and the three Hebrew young men and how God can increase your knowledge and understanding.

Guess what? He started passing test after test and then landed his dream job. It took courage for him to decide to go for it and courage to take the tests while doubting that he could pass them, but he changed his way of living and started praying and meditating on this Bible passage:

> *God shows no partiality. But in every nation whoever fears Him and works righteousness is accepted by Him.*
>
> (Acts 10:34–35)

God performed His word for that man! His courageous decision led to a better life for him and his whole family.

When pressure comes, don't give in! Go confidently in the direction of your dreams and learn to live the life God desires for you. Be bold enough to listen to your heart and have faith in God. We don't let people affect us; we affect people.

Doubt your doubts and feed your faith. The life God intended for you begins within, where you focus on thinking differently. In Proverbs 23:7, Solomon wrote these words of wisdom: *"For as he thinks in his heart, so is he."* Our thoughts and beliefs are built upon stories—the stories we tell ourselves, and what others tell us. So, be careful how you think because your life is shaped by your thoughts.

Paul emphasized the necessity of agreeing inwardly with God's law: *"For I delight in the law of God according to the inward man"* (Romans 7:22). What you agree with on the inside determines how you act on the outside. But you are not alone because Christ lives inside of us.

We must choose inwardly not to let the world affect us by rearranging our thinking in an unbiblical way. We were never meant to live in the darkness, but to be the light that diminishes the darkness and changes the atmosphere around us, just like Daniel and his three friends did.

DREAMS, A FIERY FURNACE, AND THE LION'S DEN

Daniel's complex, prophetic dreams happened at the height of his power and influence in Babylon. But before this, Daniel was put in a strange situation to interpret a dream that Nebuchadnezzar either forgot or refused to tell his advisors about. Instead, the king summoned his magicians, enchanters, sorcerers, and astrologists and told them they must describe the dream and interpret it. If they failed to do as he commanded, they would be executed.

The dream interpreters reacted in fear, saying it was impossible to interpret the dream without knowing it. So, Nebuchadnezzar ordered the killing of all the wise men in Babylon, including Daniel and his friends. When Daniel heard the news, he went to the king and told him that he would describe and interpret his dream—and so he did. The answer was a dream within a dream because Daniel dreamed the king's dream with the interpretation and saved them all. It affected the king as well; he fell before David, honored him for the interpretation, and said, "*Surely your God is the God of gods and the Lord of kings and a revealer of mysteries, for you were able to reveal this mystery*" (Daniel 2:47 NIV).

We serve a mighty God and can take a courageous stand like Daniel did. When we are brave enough to do the right thing, God will be there for us to do the miraculous.

After explaining and interpreting the king's dream, Daniel was made ruler over Babylon and chief administrator over all of its wise men, while Shadrach, Meshach, and Abed-Nego were also given high positions. (See Daniel 2:48–49.)

The good times in Babylon didn't last long, for Nebuchadnezzar made a huge golden idol and then decreed that everyone must worship this idol when music was played. Again, the three Hebrews took a courageous stand, refusing to bow before the false idol. They were then singled out and called before the infuriated king, who threatened to throw them into a fiery furnace if they did not worship the idol. (See Daniel 3:13–15.)

He was not expecting the response they gave him.

Shadrach, Meshach and Abednego replied to him, "King Nebuchadnezzar, we do not need to defend ourselves before you in this matter. If we are thrown into the blazing furnace, the God we serve is able to deliver us from it, and he will deliver us from Your Majesty's hand. But even if he does not, we want you to know, Your Majesty, that we will not serve your gods or worship the image of gold you have set up." (Daniel 3:16–18 NIV)

What a powerful statement! Whether in life or death, the three Hebrew men would remain courageous and honor God in their every action. They knew it was the correct thing to do. Their refusal to worship the image was not rooted in youthful rebellion but submission to God and His holy commandment:

"You shall have no other gods before Me" (Exodus 20:3). They put their trust in God, even though they did not know what would happen.

I don't enjoy it when people focus more on the devil than on Jesus. I could care less about all of their talk about demons in other parts of the world and the endless chatter about what the devil does. I know Jesus defeated demons and the devil and won the victory for us. We need to be like Daniel and the three Hebrew men, paying no attention to what the enemy might try to do and instead keeping our eyes locked on God.

I've heard my grandmother say, "Whatever you magnify will be magnified in your life." I don't want to magnify anything that isn't of God, especially anything the devil may be trying. He is defeated!

Another key to courage is to have complete trust in God. These three young men trusted and loved God, which made them courageous. For them, there was only one God to worship; all others were false gods. Sadly, there were many Jews who worshipped the false gods, but some remained faithful to the Almighty. We should never hesitate to take a courageous stand for God.

There was a great and glorious end to the story. Nebuchadnezzar told his soldiers to bind the three Hebrew men and throw them into the furnace, which was heated seven times hotter than it normally was. When the soldiers cast the three inside, flames were rushing from the open door with such rage that they burned the soldiers to death.

God did not deliver Daniel's friends *from* the fire, but He did deliver them *through* the fire. When King Nebuchadnezzar looked into the furnace, he was filled with astonishment at what he saw. He said to his counselors, *"Did we not cast three men bound into the midst of the fire?...I see four men loose, walking in the midst of the fire; and they are not hurt, and the form of the fourth is like the Son of God"* (Daniel 3:24–25).

The Son of God was with them in the fire! Courage is made possible when we know that we are not alone even in the most challenging times. Jesus is always with us! Whenever we face tremendous pressure to compromise our godly beliefs and values and bow before the *"god of this age"* (2 Corinthians 4:4) and secular, pagan cultural mandates, we must choose to be courageous and bold as a lion to face the enemy, no matter the situation. Some have been delivered; others made the ultimate sacrifice like Stephen, who was stoned to death by the religious leaders, or Peter, who was crucified upside down.

Nebuchadnezzar told the three Hebrew men, *"Servants of the Most High God, come out, and come here"* (Daniel 3:26). They came out and stood before the king, in the sight of all the princes, nobles, and rulers, and everyone could see that they were alive. Their garments had not been scorched, nor their hair singed, nor was there even the smell of fire upon them. (See verse 27.)

While living in this world, we should never have the scent of the secular on us, for we are the sweet fragrance of Christ.

That day in Babylon, the tide shifted in favor of the kingdom of God!

Nebuchadnezzar spoke, saying, "Blessed be the God of Shadrach, Meshach, and Abed-Nego, who sent His Angel and delivered His servants who trusted in Him, and they have frustrated the king's word, and yielded their bodies, *that they should not serve nor worship any god except their own God! Therefore I make a decree that any people, nation, or language which speaks anything amiss against the God of Shadrach, Meshach, and Abed-Nego shall be cut in pieces, and their houses shall be made an ash heap; because **there is no other God** who can deliver like this." Then the king promoted Shadrach, Meshach, and Abed-Nego in the province of Babylon.* (Daniel 3:28–30)

There is only one God, and He is Jehovah, the Lord. The whole Babylonian culture shifted from worshipping idols to worshipping God because three brave young men trusted God.

We live in a culturally problematic and perilous time, so it is our turn to be courageous and stand for what is holy and correct. Never forget that God is always with us, and He never changes; He is constantly the same yesterday, today, and forever. (See Hebrews 13:8.)

NEVER FORGET THAT GOD IS ALWAYS WITH US, AND HE NEVER CHANGES; HE IS CONSTANTLY THE SAME YESTERDAY, TODAY, AND FOREVER.

That's how we are going to change the culture around us. It's not by joining with people in the popular crowds of the world and making them fit the church. If we want a genuine friendship with God, we don't surrender to what's mainstream or easy. The path to the courage I outline in this book is the only way to go: by keeping your eyes on Jesus and trusting God in every moment. It's easy to be led astray by worldly pressures, but in these moments, we must let our light shine brightly in the dark places of ungodliness and immorality. We reject the gods of this world, and, in love, we embrace our God of power and might.

Shadrach, Meshach, and Abed-Nego lived righteous lives, yet things didn't always go so well for them. However, when they encountered evil, rather than concede like everyone else around them, they confronted their circumstances. One thing is apparent: they were fully convinced that nothing could make them bow to Nebuchadnezzar's false god. Neither threat, consequences, nor punishment would change their minds.

Trust in the Lord with all your heart! Live your life on fire for Jesus; it is the only way to live.

5

DIAMOND-CHISELING PROCESS

Among our high privileges is to radiate, to give forth
from the love-passion of our souls, the courage and
strength to help other souls to come to God.
—*John G. Lake*

"They shall be Mine," says the LORD *of hosts, "on the day
that I make them My jewels."*
—Malachi 3:17

The ancient Greeks believed that diamonds were splinters of
stars fallen to the earth. In the Greek language, the word for
diamond is *adamas*, which means "unconquerable" and "indestructible." Some cultures thought diamonds were the tears of
God.

In 327 BC, Alexander the Great brought the first diamond to Europe from India, where diamonds were first discovered. Diamonds were believed to bring strength, stop stress, and protect against fire and poison.

Diamonds are carried to the earth's surface by volcanic eruptions; very few survive the hazardous journey from the depths of the earth to reach us. The hardest of all gemstones known to man, it is also the simplest in composition, made up of only one element—carbon. In comparison, a ruby is composed of aluminum oxide with chromium. Approximately two hundred and fifty tons of ore must be mined and processed to produce a one-carat, polished, gem-quality diamond.

Why am I talking about diamonds? For one thing, God makes jewels from diamonds in the rough. He's the master gemologist, chiseling away at our rough edges, polishing us, and developing the different facets of His character, making us feel like gems in His expert hands because we allow Him to work in us.

A STORY THAT CHANGED EVERYTHING

In the first chapter of this book, I mentioned how my life was changed by the power of God and my hunger for more of Him. It turned out to be a special night at a church meeting where God touched me. And now...the rest of the story!

My sister Hannah always had a heart after God from the time she was a young girl. She would invite me to meetings and sometimes tricked me. I would suddenly discover I was in a prayer group, with people praying for me. My sister is a woman of prayer, and she knew the enemy was trying to steal my life and rob me of what God called me to do. I believe in the power of prayer; we should never stop praying for loved ones because victory is coming! By faith, we see the victory even before it manifests in the natural. My family always knew God was going to use me for His glory.

One day, my sister called me and said, "Branden, you have to go to this meeting coming up. It is only one night, and it's a revival that is happening around the country." My response was quick and firm, "No, that's okay." Being the sister she is, however, Hannah wouldn't quit. She kept calling me, saying, "Branden, please go!" Finally, I said, "Okay, I will go."

It was months before the meeting, and it was getting close to my birthday when I heard the Holy Spirit speaking to my heart again. He said, "Branden, you're getting something special for your birthday." The Spirit's message was audible, and I thought, *Maybe it's a car!* At the time, I seriously needed a car, and it was the first thing that came to my mind when I heard God's words. I was definitely not thinking about anything spiritual.

When my birthday arrived, I told my mother what the Holy Spirit had said about getting something special for my birthday. We prayed about it and moved on to other topics...until I got a call from my sister.

"Branden, tonight is the meeting, and you promised you would go," she said.

I thought, *Well, it's my birthday, but I don't want to go to church on a Friday night on my birthday.* However, I finally gave in. "Okay, let's go," I said.

I wore a tank top muscle shirt with a huge diamond on it because I had been working out a lot and wanted to show off the results.

Mom didn't like my choice of clothing. "Branden, why are you wearing that? You can't wear that!" she said.

So, I put a cardigan over the tank top, and we went to the service.

The place was so charged with expectation and the presence of God! Thousands of people had arrived, and we sat in the back. While we were waiting for the service to begin, a man came over to us and said, "We have seats for you." It turned out that our new seats were in the third row.

As the service began, I thought, *Wow, this is a long time of praise and worship, and the enemy is trying to give me a headache to make me leave.* I stayed right there.

WHEN YOU FEEL LIKE THE ENEMY IS PRESSING AGAINST YOU ON EVERY SIDE, THEN KNOW THAT YOU'RE ABOUT TO ENCOUNTER A GREAT VICTORY.

When you feel like the enemy is pressing against you on every side, then know that you're about to encounter a great victory. Once I entered full-time ministry, I experienced situations in which the enemy tried to attack me and felt that pressure.

Still, I exercised my authority and right as a believer, knowing that the victory would soon appear in Jesus's name.

If I had allowed that headache to convince me to leave that meeting, I would have missed out on what God designed for me and everything God called me to do. I know for sure I wouldn't be writing this book right now.

Never give in to pressure or anything the enemy may throw against you. He is a liar, and he lost the battle at Calvary nearly two thousand years ago. God raised Christ from the dead, and now we are seated in Christ in heavenly places.

We operate on another level—not an earthly one but a heavenly one in Jesus Christ. We don't have to submit to the devil's tricks or whatever he may try because we are seated far above him. The Father *"raised us up together, and made us sit together in the heavenly places in Christ Jesus"* (Ephesians 2:6). Jesus's victory is our victory! He won the victory for us. When you genuinely know this, not just by hearing it, but knowing it in your spirit, then you will have courage like never before. You can't live an overcomer's victory-winning walk as a believer in Christ without knowing the spiritual authority you have in Jesus Christ.

THE GRAND FINALE

While we were at the service, Hannah told me, "This guy who is ministering reminds me of you." At the time, I thought that was the funniest thing ever, but reflecting on her words again, I realize she was right because I'm now a preacher.

The minister shared his testimony and talked about the fire of God; when he was finished, he gave an invitation to anyone who needed a touch from God. People rushed to the front, but

I remained seated. My parents told me, "Branden, go down to the front!" However, I still sat there, watching the service. Suddenly, the preacher came walking toward me as people continued to rush toward him. He was pushing them aside, and the next thing I knew, he was standing in front of me.

I sensed the strong presence of God as the minister, by the Holy Spirit, started telling me all about my life, precisely what I was facing, and how God was about to change my life by the fire of the Holy Spirit! Surprisingly, he said I reminded him of himself. He continued saying that God would use me like He was using him, and there were going to be levels I would skip in ministry that took others twenty to thirty years to achieve because there is not much time left before Jesus comes back again.

The central part of the minister's word was this: "You are a diamond for God. Right now, you have some rough spots on you, but God will chisel those away, and you will shine bright for Him, and nothing will be wrong with you. You will become a flawless diamond as the Holy Spirit starts chiseling the rough spots on you."

The diamond on the tank top was showing, and the minister said, "It was no accident you wore this shirt, for God is turning you into what is on your shirt, a diamond for God, and you will shine bright for Him."

The minister started to return to the front, but then he came back and said, "You will get a revelation of this, and it will be the key to your ministry." Another part of his word was that people around me wouldn't even recognize me, and it happened the very next day. People I'd known my whole life didn't recognize me at all. It was indeed God's presence and His fire burning in my life.

What God gave me on my birthday was exactly what my grandmother, Dr. Billye Brim, told me. She said, "You didn't get a car for your birthday; you got a call from God as an evangelist." That truly is so much better than a car!

Here's another interesting facet to this whole story: my birthday is in April, and the birthstone for April is the diamond. Plus, the name Branden means "fire." It's amazing how God works! Wherever we go as we travel worldwide, Destanie and I expect the fire of God to touch every heart and life so that people are radically transformed, just as the Holy Spirit touched me that night.

THE REVELATION OF THE DIAMOND

Later, I often wondered about the revelation of the diamond that the Holy Spirit gave the minister that night, but God began to give me glimpses into its meaning. First of all, I'm not the only diamond there is in the circle of life. The Lord placed it on my heart that all of His kids are diamonds unto Him. So many Scriptures are written about how God loves us, how we are made in His image, *"fearfully and wonderfully made"* to be like Him. (See Psalm 139:14.)

We are God's diamonds, but in this earthly life, we often have our rough spots because we've been hurt, sometimes by our fellow Christians. When we embrace the inward pain, not letting go, we mar the diamonds of faith with unbelief and fail to see what God wants to do in our life.

This chiseling process applies to all of us. The secret to change is giving God His place by the power of the Holy Spirit. Your surrender is one of the tools God can use to chisel you with His cleansing fire; your life will never be the same in Jesus's name.

Let nothing hold you back. Do not hang on to any hurts. Eliminate the rough spots so you can be changed and be like the Master, Jesus, shining brightly for Him and allowing nothing to extinguish your light. It's just like the popular gospel song we sang as kids: "This little light of mine, I'm going to let it shine!" Let God's light shine through you in these days so that others can see the good things you do and glorify God. (See Matthew 5:16.) No more rough spots—in Jesus's name!

THE WONDER AND BEAUTY OF DIAMONDS

It took intense heat, pressure, and volcanic eruptions thousands of years ago to form the diamonds we see in the world today. Transitioning from the natural to the spiritual, I heard the Holy Spirit saying, "It's the same with My sons and daughters during these days." Through the heat and pressure in our lives, we are transformed into the Lord's image and then pushed to the top, where we land in the front lines. (See 2 Corinthians 3:18.) It is not by our might or power but by the energy and power of the Holy Spirit and the fire of God! He will use all of us in these last days, bringing us all out with His holy fire.

Of course, the diamonds you see at the jewelry store, all shiny and flawless, are not the diamonds in their rough state before the jeweler starts chiseling and polishing them. God is doing the same with us, chiseling and polishing us for His glory.

When you realize that you are one of God's diamonds, unconquerable and unbreakable, that should give you the courage to stand in the front lines for God. If it does not, I don't know what will. You are unbreakable because *"He who is in you is greater than he who is in the world"* (1 John 4:4). Jesus lived on this earth with an indestructible life, and we are *"more than conquerors through Him"* (Romans 8:37).

WHEN YOU REALIZE THAT YOU ARE ONE OF GOD'S DIAMONDS, UNCONQUERABLE AND UNBREAKABLE, THAT SHOULD GIVE YOU THE COURAGE TO STAND IN THE FRONT LINES FOR GOD.

The cross didn't defeat Jesus! He won the victory for us. He wasn't forced onto the cross but chose to give Himself for you and me. He could have called twelve legions of angels at any time, but He never said the word. (See Matthew 26:53.) Jesus was on a secret mission for us, doing the will of His Father, and He won us back to Him! Jesus paid it all—and we owe it all to Him. Jesus gave everything for us, and that's why we must do the same. We must give not 95 percent but 100 percent, a life on fire for God. It's not a religious duty but a celebrated relationship.

One legion is equal to six thousand, so Jesus could easily have asked the Father for 72,000 angels. One angel took out 185,000 Assyrians in one night (see 2 Kings 19:35), so twelve legions of angels could take out *more than thirteen billion* soldiers! At the time of Christ, the Roman army consisted of just 250,000 men. Even at its peak, the Roman Empire only had about 500,000 soldiers.

If the rulers of this age knew the hidden wisdom of God, *"they would not have crucified the Lord of glory"* (1 Corinthians 2:8).

While I was writing this book, I looked up from my computer and had a vision of a diamond hanging on our wall with this word underneath it: *indestructible*. What a Holy Ghost reminder of God's power in us! Every day, it is before my eyes as a constant reminder that you and I are indestructible because of what Jesus did for us. We are people of faith!

Diamonds are the hardest natural substance in our world. The only thing that can scratch a diamond is another diamond. When Saul was on the road to Damascus to persecute the church, he didn't know the force of power against him. He encountered this formidable force—the rays of glory emanating from Christ—which caused Saul to fall to the earth. While on the ground, he heard the voice of Jesus saying, *"Saul, Saul, why are you persecuting Me?"* (Acts 9:4).

When the Lord told him, *"I am Jesus, whom you are persecuting"* (verse 5), Saul realized that *"breathing threats and murder against the disciples of the Lord"* (verse 1) was the same as persecuting Christ. You cannot separate the two, for we are one in Christ. It is a good lesson to all of us because when we speak badly about any ministry or people in the body of Christ, we are talking about Jesus. Lord, forgive us in Jesus's name! Let our speech always be edifying toward the Holy Spirit and God's people, for they are unbreakable.

I have met many people as I've traveled around the world. I've seen God's people, diamonds in the rough who are precious in His sight, scratched and distressed by other people of God to the point where they leave the church. We must make a radical decision to let God's light shine without scratching others with thoughtless, hurtful words. The Bible tells us, *"Pleasant words are like a honeycomb, sweetness to the soul and health to the bones"* (Proverbs 16:24). Speak only that which is pure and of an excellent report!

King David didn't take this teaching lightly either. When the Amalekite messenger delivered the news that he had killed King Saul because he was dying anyway, David had him killed for touching God's anointed. You should never harm any of God's anointed in any way, such as talking negatively about them. I have made it a practice to pray that the Holy Spirit would put a guard over my mouth in Jesus's name.

In Isaiah 43:4, there is a word we should never forget: *"Since you were precious in My sight, you have been honored, and I have loved you."* Diamonds have been valued and coveted for thousands of years. There is evidence that diamonds were being collected and traded in India as early as the fourth century BC. In the first century AD, the Roman naturalist and philosopher Pliny the Elder reportedly said, "Diamond is the most valuable, not only of precious stones, but of all things in this world."

You are valuable and precious to God. Out of everything God created, you are his top prize, special and priceless in God's eyes. The value of something is based upon the price paid for it. *"You were not redeemed with corruptible things, like silver or gold... but with the precious blood of Christ"* (1 Peter 1:18–19).

Don't let the devil lie to you again about your worth. You're so loved and valued by God. You're God's diamond, so shine like never before.

6

THE POWER OF PRAYER

There is no sweeter manner of living in the world than
continuous communion with God.
—Brother Lawrence

The power of prayer does not flow from us. The power of prayer does not come from any extraordinary words we speak or a particular way we say them or even how often we say them. The power of prayer is not established on the precise direction we face or the position of our bodies, nor does the power of prayer come from the use of candles or beads.

The power of prayer comes from the God of power, who hears our prayers and answers.

The prayer of a godly person places us in contact with the invincible God, with tremendous results. The God to whom we pray is the source of the power of that prayer, and He answers according to His timing. God possesses the power, and prayer is a conduit to His power. Prayer is like a powerful lamp that God lights, and it illumines your darkness to encourage you and direct your prayers. An electric cord does not have power—it is just a conduit. God is all-powerful, *"for with God nothing will be impossible"* (Luke 1:37). The invitation to prayer is always available to those who seek God's support.

Jesus applied a parable to illustrate a notable truth about the power of prayer and how you should pray without giving up hope:

> *There was in a certain city a judge who did not fear God nor regard man. Now there was a widow in that city; and she came to him, saying, "Get justice for me from my adversary." And he would not for a while; but afterward he said within himself, "Though I do not fear God nor regard man, yet because this widow troubles me I will avenge her, lest by her continual coming she weary me."...Hear what the unjust judge said. And shall God not avenge His own elect who cry out day and night to Him, though He bears long with them?* (Luke 18:2–7)

COURAGE IN THE HANDS OF GOD

When we pray, fear is relieved, faith grows, peace comes, confidence is gained, prayers are answered, and God is honored. Mother Teresa of Calcutta said, "Prayer is not asking. Prayer is putting yourself in the hands of God and listening to His voice in the depth of your hearts. God shapes the world by prayer. The more praying in the world, the better the world will be, the mightier the forces against evil."

Putting yourself in the hands of the Father is the perfect place of prayer. If God is your copilot, you will find courage.

"MY DADDY'S THE PILOT"

There's a fantastic allegory that's been making the rounds for quite a few years now that illustrates the importance of knowing who is with you and who to trust on your journey. It goes like this:

> A pastor was on a long flight home after a church con-ference when the "Fasten Your Seat Belt" sign flashed on. After a while, a calm voice said, "We shall not be serving beverages at this time as we are expecting a little turbulence. Please remain seated with your seat belt fas-tened." The pastor looked around and saw that many of the passengers were becoming apprehensive.
>
> And then the storm broke.
>
> The ominous cracks of thunder could be heard even above the roar of the engines. Lightning lit up the dark-ening skies, and within moments, that great plane was tossed around like a cork in a celestial ocean. All of the passengers were alarmed…except for one little girl. She sat calmly, feet tucked under her, reading a book, seem-ingly oblivious to the turbulence around her.
>
> The storm eventually blew over. When the plane landed and the passengers were disembarking, the pastor approached the little girl and asked her how she had remained so calm during the flight. She replied, "'Cause my Daddy's the Pilot, and he's taking me home."

The power of prayer has overcome enemies, conquered death, brought healing, and defeated demons. (See Psalm 6:9–10; 2 Kings 4:32–36; James 5:14–15; Mark 9:29.) God, through prayer, opens eyes, changes hearts, heals wounds, and grants wisdom. (See Isaiah 35:5; 1 Samuel 10:9; Psalm 147:3; James 1:5.) The power of prayer should never be underestimated because it draws on the glory and might of the infinitely powerful God of the universe! Daniel 4:35 (NIV) proclaims, "*All the peoples of the earth are regarded as nothing. He does as he pleases with the powers of heaven and the peoples of the earth. No one can hold back his hand or say to him: 'What have you done?'*"

THE POWER OF PRAYER SHOULD NEVER BE UNDERESTIMATED BECAUSE IT DRAWS ON THE GLORY AND MIGHT OF THE INFINITELY POWERFUL GOD OF THE UNIVERSE!

The psalmist declares:

Then they cried out to the LORD in their trouble, and he brought them out of their distress. He stilled the storm to a whisper; the waves of the sea were hushed. They were glad when it grew calm, and he guided them to their desired haven. (Psalm 107:28–30 NIV)

THE COURAGE OF FAITH

Samson's story in Judges 13–16 reveals his complicated character from his birth until his death. Though Samson played the part of a heroic, gifted man, we cannot downplay Samson's faults and weaknesses. Even so, he died a noble death to save a nation, and he had the courage of faith to trust God with his prayer. Blinded by his enemies and bound between two pillars, Samson prayed:

> O Lord GOD, remember me, I pray! Strengthen me, I pray, just this once, O God, that I may with one blow take vengeance on the Philistines for my two eyes!…Let me die with the Philistines! (Judges 16:28–30)

And so Samson pushed against the pillars and the temple fell, killing everyone inside.

In a burst of sudden, courageous prayer empowered by his God, Samson asked the Lord to remember the reproaches cast upon him and God's people, to remember His lovingkindness, the gracious promises made to Samson, and the help and assistance he previously received from the Lord. With courage, Samson sacrificed his life for the nation he loved. While he died "with the Philistines," his faith remained fixed.

Sometimes, courage is manifested in death, as demonstrated by numerous stories through the ages.

You can pray for an increase in courage, but you can't pray for more faith because "*faith comes* by hearing, *and hearing by the word of God*" (Romans 10:17). But courage and faith emerge as the faith of courage. Faith and courage became my twin companions for overcoming obstacles and serving God in ministry.

The faith of courage enables us to advance rather than flee. Courage also defines our attitude when we approach the challenges and difficulties we encounter in our lives. Sometimes, courage is just getting up and doing what needs to be done.

When Saul initiated persecution against the church in Jerusalem, believers scattered to other parts of Judea and Samaria. (See Acts 8:1–4.) But they had faith to be courageous, so they preached the gospel when they arrived in new places, and more were saved.

After meeting Jesus on the road to Damascus and receiving the Holy Spirit after a word from Ananias, Saul the persecutor became Paul the persecuted. Sometimes, when you have the faith of courage, great things happen. Look on your adversaries with the eyes of faith; someday, by the power of God, they may be transformed from adversaries into advocates. With the apostle Paul, the word that brought persecution was the word that changed the world.

THE IMPORTANCE OF PRAYER

Prayer isn't meant to be a way to attract people's attention so that they see you are praying. That would be religious, and your motive would be wrong. In its pure form, prayer is you communicating with your heavenly Father, whether people see you or not.

To be like someone, you have to spend time with them. To be like Jesus, we need to spend time with Jesus, and we do this through prayer and communion. Choose today to pray regularly, making this your priority.

Jesus, a Man of prayer, modeled what it looked like to have a prayer life. Many times, He was up all night, having prayer time with His Father. One of my favorite verses in the Bible is this one:

Very early in the morning, while it was still dark, Jesus got up, left the house and went off to a solitary place, where he prayed. (Mark 1:35 NIV)

There is something so special about getting away from distractions and the noise of life so that you can pray. Jesus could have stayed in bed to recover from His grueling ministry or the multiple distractions from the religious leaders. Instead, He guarded His time to be with His Father, going off by Himself to the private places of a mountain or the wilderness to pray.

To be a powerful and anointed preacher, you must make prayer a regular priority, for prayer refreshes your spirit and provides your agenda for the day. I believe that for Jesus, life in the secret place of prayer empowered Him for His public ministry. I'm a young minister, and God has blessed our ministry with unusual blessings that have been genuinely supernatural. But my number one key for my life is my commitment to prayer.

My prayer life reminds me that God is my source, so I don't have to rely on what I can do or what my family can do, but on what God can do through me. Being alone in prayer calms my soul and gives me peace, as I know God is with me in those private times. During prayer, God reveals things about my life and what He will do, and I trust Him. Those times of prayer give me the courage to be faithful to my call and confident in Him.

Once, when I was backstage at a meeting with other ministers, they were talking about what they were doing, trying to impress me or each other. I just smiled and loved on them with the love of Jesus. As a young man, it would be easy for me to boast about what I have done, but I know it is all about God. I put my confidence in God and not myself because I can't do anything without Him.

Jesus is my example, and I choose to follow Him.

Take My yoke upon you and learn from Me, for I am gentle and lowly in heart, and you will find rest for your souls.
(Matthew 11:29)

Jesus's life of prayer challenges me to have more time dedicated to prayer with God. I'm so hungry for more of Jesus, to know Him and His ways like many of you do, *"that I may know Him and the power of His resurrection"* (Philippians 3:10).

Every second of the day, we discover ways to know more about Jesus and His resurrection power. There are no limits to what we must learn; it is a lifetime of discoveries. Prayer is founded on God's Word, not on our thoughts and ideas. The Word of God has to be our foundation in our life of prayer.

PRAYING WITH THE SCRIPTURES IS AN INVALUABLE WAY TO PRAY BECAUSE YOU CAN TURN A VERSE INTO A PRAYER AND DECLARATION.

Praying with the Scriptures is an invaluable way to pray because you can turn a verse into a prayer and declaration. As you pray, you will get a download from the Holy Spirit, giving you courage like you never imagined.

Praying for courage for myself changed my life. When preaching, I often feel a surge of courage being imparted and removing any heaviness or struggles the listeners may be experiencing. The Word of God never returns void, for it is *"living and powerful, and sharper than any two-edged sword"* (Hebrews 4:12).

I have a story that validates my words on prayer. I was asked to preach for my friend Dr. Larry Ollison at the Walk on the Water Faith Church in Osage Beach, Missouri. I shared a testimony on being courageous, and God moved mightily in that service. As I concluded the service, the whole crowd rose to their feet, cheered, and then worshipped God. That's the first time my preaching ever received that kind of response. But God spoke, telling me that courage was being imparted into the lives of those people during the service, and they were giving God the glory.

After the service, while I was in the back getting refreshments, the pastor and his lovely wife walked in. He said, "Branden, we never saw what just happened ever in our church, ever," referring to the standing ovation.

Then he shared that many people in his congregation were dealing with the death of loved ones. The preaching of God's Word and the anointing that followed caused people who were saddened to start jumping up and down, freed with godly courage to live again. The Word of God affected many that night, and an impartation of courage with joy was the result.

CATALYTIC POWER OF UNITY AND PRAYER

The apostles in the early church had everything stacked against them. Opposition to the Christian faith was rampant, with disciples being thrown into jail, harassed, threatened again and again, and killed. Despite the opposition, the early church grew by the catalytic force of unity and prayer, resulting in notable exhibitions of worship. After healing a lame man in the name of Jesus, Peter and John told the rulers they could not keep silent.

> *And being let go, they went to their own companions and reported all that the chief priests and elders had said to them.* (Acts 4:23)

Where else would you go except to the company of friends who love God and one another? There is power in unity. God calls the church to be a vibrant and powerful one that bears much fruit, and the way we do that is by working together in perfect unity, not through faultless doctrine, seamless systems, flawless worship services, or impeccable leadership. We are likened to a body because unity in diversity gets things done.

> *Just as a body, though one, has many parts, but all its many parts form one body, so it is with Christ.*
> (1 Corinthians 12:12 NIV)

After hearing from Peter and John, the people of the early church raised their voices to God in prayer with one accord and received a decisive outcome.

> *"Now, Lord, look on their threats, and grant to Your servants that with all boldness they may speak Your word, by*

stretching out Your hand to heal, and that signs and won-ders may be done through the name of Your holy Servant Jesus." And when they had prayed, the place where they were assembled together was shaken; and they were all filled with the Holy Spirit, and they spoke the word of God with boldness. (Acts 4:29–31)

The power of prayer will rock every boat, open every door, and dramatically release the power of God with holy boldness and manifestations of signs and wonders in Jesus's name.

"And when they had prayed, the place… was shaken." The event that followed was evidence that God heard their prayer. The place where they had gathered was shaken as though there was an earthquake. It was proof of the presence and power of God.

"They were all filled with the Holy Spirit." It was like another Pentecost, and this blend of the Holy Spirit with the human spirit created an acceleration of spiritual power and church growth.

"They spoke the word of God with boldness." They boldly preached the gospel of the kingdom with great freedom and without fear, not only privately but also in public, in the streets and in the temple.

THE SEASON OF PRAYER AND BOLDNESS

I was once in Washington State to preach in a small town that was utterly ungodly. Churches in this town were not typical at all, for it was a very unchurched region. We were there for three days and nights, and on the first night, I preached from Acts 4 about miracles and courage. In that meeting, there was a lovely young lady in her forties with a beautiful smile, who went to the front of the church, asking for prayer. I noticed right away that one of her eyes was entirely shut from having a stroke. I knew she was hoping to be healed.

I had finished preaching about miracles and the healing power in the name of Jesus, so I laid my hands on her damaged eye and prayed. I declared the healing power and authority in Jesus's name, and as soon as I declared it, she was instantly healed. Immediately, she started yelling, "I'm healed! I'm healed!"

That sweet lady's testimony went around that town, and many other people came for a heavenly touch and miracle from God. Another lady told me that if God had not touched her that night, she would have killed herself. That town saw and heard what was happening in the church and the stories of how people experienced the miraculous healing power of Jesus.

What God did through the apostles and the early church, He can do in our days! In those early days of the church, after the ascension of Jesus, prayer was prominent, primary, and imperative for their existence and expansion. They were spiritual warriors advancing the kingdom of God. The opposition commanded them not to speak or teach, but they boldly proclaimed God's Word.

With these classic words, Peter healed the lame man at the temple gate:

> *Silver and gold I do not have, but what I do have I give you: In the name of Jesus Christ of Nazareth, rise up and walk.*
>
> (Acts 3:6)

And the man *"stood and walked and entered the temple with them—walking, leaping, and praising God"* (verse 8).

The miracle caused an uproar, filling everyone who had witnessed it with wonder and amazement. It gave the apostles an opportunity to preach the gospel to the crowds with even greater boldness. On the day of Pentecost, three thousand were saved, and on this day, five thousand more were saved.

Now that is a genuine revival unlike any today! They didn't need a massive tent, a colossal auditorium, or thousands of dollars. But these are different times, and many have impacted the kingdom through bold preaching and miracles.

There is an intriguing testimony about God's power and the apostles' boldness.

> *Now when they saw the boldness of Peter and John, and perceived that they were uneducated and untrained men, they marveled. And they realized that they had been with Jesus.*
>
> (Acts 4:13)

The boldness of Jesus's speech was now evident in Peter and John, who were filled with courage and felt free to speak. Another thing that stood out was their lack of education. The scribes and religious leaders trained under the great Jewish scholars, but they were stunned by the apostles' ability to unveil the Old Testament Scriptures and present the life and message of Jesus in such a compelling way.

Finally, they sensed that these two men had been with Jesus. Their boldness, preaching, and power set them apart from others, but there was something else, something special. Their presence and speech linked them to Jesus. The religious leaders might have said to themselves, "We thought we got rid of Him, but look! He reappears in these men, and what troubled us in the Nazarene now annoys and frustrates us with people like Him." What a testimony to these witnesses!

THE SCRIBES AND RELIGIOUS LEADERS WERE STUNNED BY THE APOSTLES' ABILITY TO UNVEIL THE OLD TESTAMENT SCRIPTURES AND PRESENT THE LIFE AND MESSAGE OF JESUS IN SUCH A COMPELLING WAY.

Would that the same could be said of us!

Spending time in His presence enables us to follow in His footsteps and be like Jesus—bold, loving, commanding, convincing, courageous, and powerful. Not by education alone, not by might nor power, but by His Spirit. (See Zechariah 4:6.) The Holy Spirit makes Jesus real to people and also gives you courage. Before Jesus's death, He told His disciples that He would not leave us as orphans but would send the Holy Spirit to be alongside us, empowering us and gifting us to advance God's purpose. (See John 14:16–18.) The explosion of Holy Ghost power demonstrated with signs and wonders was the launching pad for changing the world.

SPEAK WITH COURAGE

Paul told the church at Ephesus:

Pray also that God's revelation would be released through me every time I preach the wonderful mystery of the hope-filled gospel. Yes, pray that I may preach the wonderful news of God's kingdom with bold freedom at every opportunity. Even though I am chained as a prisoner, I am his ambassador. (Ephesians 6:19–20 TPT)

In critical situations, when you have a significant opportunity, you ask for prayer, so what you say is confidently spoken and intelligibly communicated in a way that the hearer is noticeably influenced. The direct focus of Paul's prayer was that the word given as his mouth is opened would be a word of wisdom by the Spirit. Paul's situation was life-threatening, yet he prayed not for the right words to defend himself before the imperial court, but that he might courageously share the mystery of the gospel.

Do not depend on your eloquence but upon spiritual impartation to touch the hearer's heart. The shortest road to any soul is by way of heaven, praying to God to open the door and your mouth, availing yourself of every opening, which is what Paul did throughout his ministry.

In whatever opportunity you have to influence someone, speak without hesitation. Boldly and freely convey the Word of God, and perhaps you can change someone's life for the better. Speak from your heart to touch the soul. *You must do what you think you cannot do; that is the moment to be bold as a lion.* When you stop to look fear in its face, you grow in strength, courage, and composure with each experience you encounter.

"The wicked flee when no one pursues, but the righteous are bold as a lion" (Proverbs 28:1). Being afraid of one's own shadow

creates a sense of unreasonable timidity, and in some circum-stances, people become fearful for no reason. When we face actual events requiring bravery, that is the time to act. Let your life be an advertisement of your strength and courage found in God's grace and power.

The righteous ones are those who trust in the Lord—the ones who have faith and place their hope on the mercy, power, and wisdom of God. Martin Luther's life was one long act of lionhearted boldness against the abuses of the Roman church for the glory of the gospel. His most famous stand took place in 1521 at a kind of trial in the city of Worms before the Roman emperor, the local governor, the archbishop of Trier, and a host of lords and princes. This assembly of influential people who could execute Luther would be enough to cause fear in anyone, but not Luther. When the prosecutor asked him if he would repudiate his books and the errors they contained, Luther boldly replied:

> Unless I am convinced by the testimony of Scripture or by clear reason (for I trust neither pope nor coun-cil alone, since it is well known that they have often erred and contradicted themselves), I am bound by the Scriptures I have cited, for my conscience is captive to the Word of God. I cannot and will not recant any-thing, since to act against one's conscience is neither safe nor right. I cannot do otherwise. Here I stand, may God help me.[11]

11. Eric W. Gritsch, "1521 The Diet of Worms," Christian History Institute, *Christian History* magazine No. 28, "100 Most Important Events in Church History"; christianhistoryinstitute.org/magazine/article/diet-of-worms.

We are the righteousness of God, so we should be as bold as a lion. Our Savior, the Lion of the tribe of Judah, does not back down.

Begin to pray and speak over yourself, "I'm bold as a lion!" If Paul prayed for courage and boldness, you can also pray that same prayer. Before I even started preaching publicly, I knew I needed to be brave enough to preach the truth. But courage and boldness are not just for preachers; all of us should be unflinching in every life situation.

IF YOU BELIEVE, YOU WILL RECEIVE

When you pray for courage, whether you feel a difference or not, you will receive it by faith. You walk by faith, not by feelings. You trust and have faith that God will make you bold when you are confronted in challenging places. The brave ones do not bounce up and down like a yo-yo, but are steadfast and do not shrivel in the face of fear.

For assuredly, I say to you, whoever says to this mountain, "Be removed and be cast into the sea," and does not doubt in his heart, but believes that those things he says will be done, he will have whatever he says. Therefore, I say to you, whatever things you ask when you pray, believe that you receive them, and you will have them. (Mark 11:23–24)

It is the *faith of God* that moves mountains. It is not our faith, but God's gift of faith to us. It's a strong belief that God can accomplish things that appear to be difficult with infinite ease, as when Jesus made the fig tree wither away with a word. (See verses 14, 21.) Another translation of Jesus's message to pray with the faith of God says, *"Believe that you have received it, and it will be yours"* (NIV).

I'm bold for Jesus. I started praying and declaring I had courage when I saw no evidence, even when it seemed like I had none. Once you have prayed that prayer of faith, don't go back and say, "Well, I hope it worked." No, you declare it because you now have courage and boldness. *"Now faith is the substance of things hoped for, the evidence of things not seen"* (Hebrews 11:1). Faith is the primary support system for all we hope for and the persuasive demonstration of invisible things. You may not see it, but it still exists. It might be hidden from your eyes at the moment, but it will be revealed when it's necessary.

LIVING THE LIMITLESS LIFE

If you don't have faith to see the unseen things God wants to do, then you will live a life of limitations. But when you have faith in God for courage, the possibilities are endless.

I'm determined I will never let anyone limit the opportunities available to me. A Latin expression you may know is *carpe diem*, which means "seize the day." I want to be someone who seizes the day with courage. I have faith in the only God who has no limits!

To live a limitless life, one must avoid having a victim mindset or being double-minded. I know people who limit themselves because they did not have a father or mother to help build their faith, which makes me sad, and I am thankful for those who overcome those limitations created by disadvantages. I am grateful that my faith was not limited but was strengthened by my heritage, and my image of God is one of an almighty God!

Think about the story of Jacob's favorite son, Joseph, in Genesis 37–39. Though his brothers threw him in a pit and then sold him into Egyptian slavery, he never allowed his faith in God to waver even while in prison.

Avoid the victim mindset and embrace the faith mindset that brings you to the ultimate breakthrough. When you ask in faith, you will receive.

> Let him **ask in faith**, with no doubting, for he who doubts is like a wave of the sea driven and tossed by the wind. For let not that man suppose that he will receive anything from the Lord; he is a double-minded man, unstable in all his ways.
>
> (James 1:6–8)

Double-mindedness, like brainwashing, distorts reality so that a person cannot see accurately. No one can expect to live a victorious life if they are unstable, for they cannot spiritually perceive what God has for them. Stability comes from trusting God with the whole heart.

When you have the mind of Christ, you see clearly because of faith in God. Don't listen to the doubters and naysayers. Considering the wrong voices makes you twisted in your thinking. Be fully persuaded that when you pray, God hears you and answers you.

When Lazarus died, Jesus first prayed and thanked God that His Father heard Him, and then He raised His friend from the dead. (See John 11:41–44.)

Reflecting on the right voices and God's Word provides an accurate perspective of any situation.

When the Assyrians were encamped against Jerusalem, King Hezekiah of Judah told his people:

> *"Be strong and courageous. Do not be afraid or discouraged because of the king of Assyria and the vast army with him, for there is a greater power with us than with him. With him is only the arm of flesh, but with us is the* Lord *our God to help us and to fight our battles." And the people gained confidence from what Hezekiah the king of Judah said.* (2 Chronicles 32:7–8 NIV)

Weak, frail, mortal men should not be feared because nothing compares with Yahweh, our God and Lord. Hezekiah assured his people that God was on their side, giving them the strength and power of the Lord and making them bold, though the battle was yet to be won.

You might remember from the last chapter that just one angel wiped out that Assyrian army! There is always more *for* us and *with* us than is with the enemy. *"He who is in you is greater than he who is in the world"* (1 John 4:4). As children of the Most High God, we should never be fearful or frightened of the enemy. Never! We need to have that awareness of God's presence with us. The enemy has *"only the arm of flesh,"* while we have our mighty God. We've got them outnumbered because Jehovah is on our side.

Which would you rather have, physical or spiritual strength? The late UCLA basketball coach John Wooden often said, "Physical strength is measured by what one can carry; spiritual strength by what one can bear." By being a man of faith himself and encouraging his players to have a robust belief system,

Wooden developed players with both physical strength and spiritual strength.

There is only one life, the limitless life, *"for in Him we live and move and have our being"* (Acts 17:28). God is the original fountain and source of life; all the qualities and capacities of a vigorous, thriving life are in Him, making us physically and spiritually alive. Even to perform the slightest motion, we depend entirely on Him for strength and power to be bold like a lion. He supports us every moment. He sustains us by His powerful Word, and we cannot exist without the courageous life found in the faith of God.

We find this life in the secret place of prayer. Your prayers might not be fancy, but they are effective nonetheless. As Max Lucado would say, "Our prayers may be awkward. Our attempts may be feeble. But since the power of prayer is in the one who hears it and not in the one who says it, our prayers do make a difference."

7

HEAVENLY VISION

Our courage must rise higher than ever, and we must
abandon ourselves more completely to the Lord,
so that His mighty power may the more perfectly work
in us all the good pleasure of His will.
—*Hannah Whitall Smith*

Before I had a heavenly vision and understanding of genuine courage, I needed to make a pivotal decision in my life that would affect my future and what God had in store for me. God has a plan for all His children and a special calling for everyone, but we still have to say "yes" to His plan, and this is where courage is needed. When God created us, He didn't create robots to say and do everything perfectly as if we were programmed. Instead, God gave us a will, a brain to think, and the Holy Spirit living inside us as an assistant to help guide us in life, just as Jesus promised. (See John 16:7.)

Satan provides a perfect example of one who used free will to make the wrong decisions. He chose not to worship God, and in his pride, he exalted himself. The Lord said, "*You were perfect in your ways from the day you were created, till iniquity was found in you*" (Ezekiel 28:15). Making that decision to rebel was also disastrous for one-third of the angels, who chose to follow Satan.

When your mind and spirit are flooded with things contradicting God's Word, things that are not edifying, as days become weeks, weeks become months, and then years pass, your spirit is weakened, and your flesh takes control. Such internal deterioration of the soul affects the decisions you make in life, so that instead of experiencing God's best for you, you are fed by the devil's fruit.

AT FIRST, CHOOSING YOUR WILL OVER GOD'S WILL
MIGHT SEEM FUN, BUT IN THE END,
THE DEVIL WILL STEAL FROM YOU, KILL YOU, OR
DESTROY EVERYTHING YOU HOLD DEAR.

My family always told me, even when I was a kid, "Don't ever eat the devil's bread," but they never told me what that meant. So I developed my own interpretation of that warning: if what you're doing doesn't glorify God, more than likely, you're eating the devil's bread. At first, it may seem sweet and feel good to your flesh, but in the end, you will be damaged because it's pulling you away from your Savior.

The enemy only wants to steal, kill, and destroy, as John 10:10 says. At first, choosing your will over God's will might seem fun, but in the end, the devil will steal from you, kill you, or destroy everything you hold dear.

THE NEED FOR A FATHER

From a human viewpoint, I didn't have much of a father growing up. My parents separated when I was only five, so I never knew what it felt like to have a father figure in my life. But I sensed God filling that void. We serve a good God who is also our Father and loves us so much. Throughout His ministry, Jesus declared and demonstrated His Father's heart of love. Jesus knew God as the good shepherd who seeks the lost sheep and the loving Father waiting on the porch for the prodigal son to come home. Christ desires that we should know and love His Father as Jesus does so that we can experience intimacy with the Father, crying out, "Abba, Papa."

Although my human father wasn't there for me, our heavenly Father was, and I experienced His love. When I was fifteen years old, I was preparing to play a game of basketball, but when I glanced in the mirror, I realized I should shave. But I didn't know how.

In the movies, you often see the classic scene of a father teaching his son how to shave—applying shaving cream, carefully scraping the whiskers off, occasionally putting the razor blade under the faucet to wash it off, and then finishing up. My life was nothing like that. Not having a father to teach me, I taught myself, endeavoring to shave but not really knowing what to do. However, when I was done, all of my facial hair was gone—and I didn't even cut myself!

COURAGE TO MAKE THE BIG DECISION

There was a time when the enemy was trying to steal everything God had planned for me, and I needed divine intervention. I was never one to share about the times of testing in my life, but I was desperately crying out to Him in private. "God, I need You! I need help." I wasn't always 100 percent on fire for God, but I never took my eyes off of my Father, so I have an excellent grasp of God as my Father.

While I was calling out to God for help, I heard these words in my spirit, ringing clear as a bell: "Branden, I'm not just your spiritual Father but also your earthly Father, and I taught you how to shave, and you didn't even know it." Wow! Stunned and overwhelmed with God's love, I sat there, knowing God is my Father—not only my Father but *your* Father also. This alone should fill you with courage.

One night, while I was preaching at a youth summer camp, I felt compelled to share the story about how God is our spiritual Father and our earthly Father who loves us so much. That night, a fifteen-year-old young man got saved and was touched by the Holy Spirit. God's love changed his life.

The next day at church, his grandmother told me his life story. She said his parents never raised him; they abandoned him at a very young age and coerced him to live with his grandparents. This young man was hurting so bad that he took it out on other people. When his grandparents insisted he go to church with them that night, he decided to shave for the first time. Like me, he was sad because he didn't have his father around to help him shave.

The story I shared radically impacted him and made him give his life to Jesus! He knew he didn't have that father figure in real life, but God wasn't just his spiritual Father—He was this young man's earthly Father, too. Now he sings praises to God all day in the house! How amazing is that? Knowing God's love for you will impact you and enable you to live a life of joy.

HEARING FROM GOD

When I cried out to God for help, there was a pivotal decision I needed to make in my life. I had been dating a girl for over two years, and our relationship was ultimately against what God had in store for me. I could sense God leading me to break the relationship, but I lacked the courage to do it. This girl was totally against my serving God and against my family's ministry, and she didn't believe in the way I was brought up.

I felt such anxiety from being in this relationship and knowing it wasn't God's best for me that my body broke out with shingles. I went to see my doctor, who told me, "Branden, I've never seen someone have shingles at your age, and it could only come from extreme stress and pressure."

Boom! I now knew what the problem was, so I immediately prayed, and the very next day, the shingles were completely gone, which was a miracle.

At the same time, the relationship I was in was also a comfortable place, with big promises for the future. Still, that future would not be in ministry, which was the opposite of what God had planned for me. I was locked in a tug of war and feeling conflicted. The questions were flying through my mind. *Do I stay and enjoy the comfortable place but forsake what God has in store for me? Or do I break this relationship, knowing it's not what God has planned for my life? Did God truly call me to be in ministry?* These thoughts plagued me. I knew my family was called to be in ministry, but at the same time, the enemy was saying, "You're not called, so stay where you are."

However, the Holy Spirit said, "No, you're called by God, so trust Me."

Sometimes when you're in a comfortable place, it's hard to courageously make the difficult decision. It seems like everything will be easier if you just remain where you are. I knew that ending the relationship would shift and affect my whole future. As I was in that battle, crying out to God for help and guidance, I began to read the Bible a lot. This is where we need to go in tough times, turning to the Word of God.

I remembered something I heard Dr. Kenneth Hagin say: "The Bible is God speaking to you." I went to the Word for support and encouragement, which I desperately needed. Knowing what I know now, I realize that the Holy Spirit directed me to study the subject of courage, and I became consumed with the matter. It seemed like I saw the word "courage" everywhere in the Bible. I started to pray for boldness, asking God to give me the courage I needed to make the right decision.

MAKING THE RIGHT CHOICE

One evening, I had a vision from God in which I was sitting in my car at a gas station and saw a beautiful picture of a road, which I knew was about my life. In the distance, there was a split in the road, with sharp turns to the left and right. God said, "You know what to do. If you decide to stay in this relationship, it's not My perfect will for your life, for you will be headed to the left side of the road."

Then I heard Him say, "My love for you won't ever change, but you will not know My blessings and the best I had for you in your life if you go down that road. But the road I have for you is the right side of the road, and you will know and experience My blessings and love like never before."

I knew I had to make that decision immediately and make the right turn, but I also knew it would require great courage to step out of the comfortable place where I was situated.

A JOURNEY TO HEAVEN

Shortly after that, on a typical afternoon, I was lying on the couch with my eyes closed, worshipping God. Sometimes when you feel stressed or under intense pressure, the best thing you can do is worship God, so that's what I was doing, just like Paul and Silas did while they were praising God in prison in Acts 16:25. I was in a situation where I also felt trapped, so I was worshipping God with all my heart. I felt God's presence so strong, like an intense heat on my chest. It felt like an anointing consuming my entire being. I began to open my eyes slowly and was startled when I saw two angels.

The first angel looked right at me, with a beautiful smile. The other angel was looking away from me and was holding a stack of papers about two feet high. The first angel grabbed a piece of paper from the stack and laid it on my chest. This paper formed against my chest like wet papier-mâché, and I sensed heat from it.

I was immediately taken up to a bright place that I knew was heaven. I wasn't in a dream-like state, but was making decisions to walk wherever I wanted. To make sure it wasn't a dream, I tested my surroundings, walking to the left, sharply turning, stopping, and then walking to the right and jumping up and down. Then, I started walking toward a beautiful park I saw in the distance. When I approached the park, I noticed benches where you could sit. There was a perfect path of trees on either side, and I would say they were about one hundred feet high. Each tree on the road seemed to be lit up by light itself. I even passed other people as I walked.

I didn't feel alarmed or scared but felt such peace and freedom. I sensed this was a heavenly encounter, and I wanted to enjoy this moment and take it all in. I felt like I was home where I belonged. Neither my present home in California nor my former home in Missouri can begin to compare with what I felt there. In my spirit, I detected this was my true home.

Doesn't the Bible say that to us? Earth isn't our final home; heaven is where we will spend eternity. Jesus said, *"In My Father's house are many mansions…I go to prepare a place for you"* (John 14:2). The day-to-day life here on earth is nothing like heaven. In addition to the wondrous beauty that I was seeing, my mind could think and comprehend amazing things.

While I was visiting heaven, I had such an intense desire to learn more about God and His ways. When I thought of heaven as a young boy, I thought we would be there playing harps, but I can tell you we will be learning about God and His ways and working on a supernatural level forever.

**WHEN I THOUGHT OF HEAVEN AS A YOUNG BOY,
I THOUGHT WE WOULD BE THERE PLAYING HARPS, BUT
INSTEAD, WE WILL BE LEARNING ABOUT GOD
AND HIS WAYS AND WORKING ON A
SUPERNATURAL LEVEL FOREVER.**

I left the park and saw a big glass door open as I approached it. Inside was a small classroom filled with seated students who looked like the people I had passed as I was walking in the park. They looked at me and told me to sit down so the class could begin.

I thought, *Maybe I shouldn't have taken that walk in the park since I'm late for class.* Eventually, I took my seat in the front center row, which was the only seat available. It seemed like the chair was waiting for me. The first thing I did was look behind me. There were about fifty people in the classroom. It was all white with long tables and ten people in each row. All of us were wearing white tunic gowns that ended right above our ankles. I still remember the face of the lady who sat right behind me. She was in her early thirties, with dark, shoulder-length hair and beautiful brown eyes.

There was a huge, serious, and strong-looking angel standing by the front door that I just had walked through. He was around twelve feet tall, wearing all white. His face was glowing, and he had short blonde hair.

In front of the classroom was a huge whiteboard with a wooden door on it, a back-entrance type of door with a golden doorknob.

That door flung open, and the speaker walking through it brought joy and much laughter. I knew the speaker was King David! And I knew the angel standing by the front door was King David's personal angel. David had a groomed beard and was a little muscular, with olive-colored skin and reddish-brown hair. He had a joyful spirit and was not formal or stiff at all.

I was reminded of Psalm 100:2, *"Serve the LORD with gladness."* King David demonstrated to me what that looked like. Being very joyful and happy was such a significant part of this vision.

A dear friend who's a pastor in Oklahoma was wonderfully ministered to when I shared this vision. He had been facing a big battle concerning his health. What helped him the most in his trying time was remembering what I said about King David being informal and full of heavenly joy. Now my friend is 100 percent healthy, for which I praise God!

The first thing King David said was, "Today I'm going to teach you on courage." His voice was loud and powerful, and he wrote the word "courage" on the whiteboard with a purple marker in beautiful cursive. What a perfect heavenly teacher on the subject! David is a prime example in the Bible of someone who lived a courageous life and trusted God at all times.

He immediately declared, "There is a test coming," as his angel proceeded to quickly pass out the test. The angel also handed me four big books concerning the subject of courage. The test appeared to be about seven pages long, with about fifty multiple choice questions. Thank God it was multiple choice! As I looked over the test, the class was dismissed, but before the people fled out of the classroom, David again declared, "A test is coming!"

Getting out of my chair, I picked up the books and started to walk out of the classroom. While I waited behind a few people in front of me, I wondered what was going to happen next. Then, I noticed David was in front of me to my right. I even noticed the sandals he was wearing. As I got closer to David, I didn't want to bother him, so I slowly walked past him by the angel, who was on my left side next to the front door. The angel sternly grabbed me and handed something to me that I had never seen before. It looked like a bizarre, oversized pen covered in white gold, but it was shaped differently than a typical pen.

As I was walking out the glass door, David came up behind me, and I felt him putting his arm around me, hugging me and laughing. David was so full of love it seemed to be radiating off him. David said, "I'll tell you what that is in your hand," as we were walking out of the classroom past hundreds of people who were waiting to get inside.

David was dressed like royalty in a white robe outlined in purple, and he put on a gold crown. He said to me, "Let's get away from all these people." We walked toward a park bench that was in a clear area off in the distance.

I was carrying the pen-type thing and a few books. David said, "These books are not for you yet, but while you're here, that thing in your hand is a highlighter, and whatever you choose to highlight, it will be in pure gold, and only your eyes will see it."

There was more to the vision, which I'll share in the next chapter, but what struck me the most—when I came back to my body and opened my eyes—was an increase in strength and courage like I'd never sensed before. I felt like a new man! With this new godly courage, I realized, *I'm still in a relationship, and I'm not supposed to be with her.*

You should never overlook or ignore the checks the Holy Spirit may give you about another person. Ignoring any reservations you are feeling never leads to anything good. God can bring the best person for your life, just like He did with me when he brought my wife Destanie to me as I focused on Jesus and Him alone.

So, I experienced an upsurge in courage, and I made the right decision to end that relationship, which became a key to my future life. God answered the cry of my heart by giving me the courage to make the right decision, be in ministry, and discover everything God had for me.

I called my grandmother to let her know. Then, while I was looking in the mirror, I heard the Holy Spirit speak to me loudly, saying, "Branden, you passed the test. It wasn't a test on paper, but you are making that decision to end that relationship." I passed! I'm so thankful I did.

I pray this vision blesses you and helps you understand that courage is God-given. There's even a special class on courage in heaven. God wants you and me to have courage, and it's time for us to take it seriously and never be discouraged another day in our lives.

Throughout the Bible, we're urged to be courageous. Let's have courage like never before. The next chapter is a class on new beginnings!

8

NEW BEGINNINGS

Be of good courage, and rest quietly in the Lord. God
can make the sun rise in the west if He pleases, and He
can make your source of distress the channel of delight.
—*Charles H. Spurgeon*

Joel prophesied, "*I will pour out My Spirit on all flesh; your
sons and your daughters shall prophesy, your old men shall dream
dreams, your young men shall see visions*" (Joel 2:28). Hundreds
of years later, after the Holy Spirit descended upon those in
the upper room, Peter addressed the crowds and repeated Joel's
prophecy.

We live in these last days, and the spiritual realm will leak
over into this natural realm as we live in daily expectation of
more heavenly encounters. We are human beings having a
supernatural experience, as Pierre Teilhard de Chardin said.

In a real sense, we are supernatural, having been born by the breath of God and made in His image. There is nothing weird about that. Most Christians and believers fail to realize this powerful truth that we live in this world physically but live supernaturally from another realm.

Brother Kenneth E. Hagin powerfully expressed how the supernatural should be natural:

> But as you walk with the Lord, as you prepare your heart, as you feed upon His word, as you listen to what the Spirit of God says, your heart shall be prepared, and your mind will be changed until you flow in the supernatural as naturally as a bird flies through the air. And you'll flow in the supernatural as naturally as a fish will swim in the water. And you'll flow in the supernatural as naturally as you breathe the very air.[12]

Jesus even said His disciples *"are not of the world, just as I am not of the world"* (John 17:16). We are the salt of the earth, reflectors of the divine nature, called to be different, resisting the moral decay in the world and set apart for God's purposes. In Ephesians 2:6, Paul refers to the believers as seated with Christ in heavenly places, positioned in the spirit realm above spiritual forces. Paul's language is supernatural, and it shouldn't be strange to us, for these words echo who we are.

I love hearing powerful men and women of God share their amazing stories. You can hear a common thread of supernatural experiences. Their stories of the supernatural indicate that they are not of the natural realm but have *tapped into the spirit realm.*

---

12. "Flowing in the Supernatural: Prophecy through Kenneth E. Hagin in 1980," Billye Brim Ministries, August 17, 2020; billyebrim.org/flowing-in-the-supernatural-kenneth-e-hagin-1980.

IT'S THE SPIRITUALLY MINDED WHO PRESERVE THIS WORLD FROM ITS DECOMPOSING ELEMENTS.

Yet this overused adage leads to a wrong conclusion of life in the Spirit. Some say, "Don't be so spiritually minded that you're no earthly good." However, it's the spiritually minded who preserve this world from its decomposing elements. The spiritually minded separate themselves from other people and even other Christians and ministers who are striving to be important in man's eyes, constantly competing with others. Those who are spiritual experience perfect peace, enjoying the rest of God. When you live the supernatural lifestyle, instead of striving, you are thriving, and you are completing one another rather than competing with others. Spiritually minded people are the ones you can trust.

When I wrote this book while being led by the Lord, He told me exactly what to do and how it would be released. I realized I was not alone as I wrote, and my thoughts ascended above my natural mindset. Many people might think I am crazy, but being spiritually minded is the lifestyle I embrace and enjoy. I knew if God said it, He would do it, even when it took more time and did not happen the way that I thought it would. After I finished writing, I waited for more than two years to see what to do next.

THE SPIRITUALLY MINDED

I didn't know anything about writing, nor did I know anyone who could help me. I didn't know any publishers either. But I knew God, and when I heard His voice tell me to write and how this book would be released, I had to think higher and say, "Yes, Lord!" This is being spiritually minded, not limited by the natural mind and its reasoning. When we tap into God's realm, nothing will shift us to unbelief, for with God, nothing is impossible. The unseen world is our home, and if God is for us, who can be against us? Nothing!

Even when I hear about ministries sowing a large amount of money, I don't envy it or get mad, but I just think, *Wow, that is not normal; it is supernatural.* God wants us to give by sowing supernaturally and receiving at a supernatural level.

Comparing the natural with the spiritual, Paul wrote:

The natural man does not receive the things of the Spirit of God, for they are foolishness to him; nor can he know them, because they are spiritually discerned.

(1 Corinthians 2:14)

The natural man is dominated by pure intellectual reasoning and natural affections; he is incapable of understanding or accepting the things of the spirit, for they belong to those who are people of the Spirit.

Those who live in the Spirit are able to carefully evaluate all things, and they are subject to the scrutiny of no one but God.　　　　(1 Corinthians 2:15 TPT)

The spiritual mind has been enlightened by the Spirit of God, assisting us to perceive and comprehend what others cannot.

In Paul's letters to the churches in Corinth and Rome, he addressed the subject of our three minds: natural, carnal, and spiritual. He wrote, *"For to be carnally minded is death, but to be spiritually minded is life and peace"* (Romans 8:6). We need to think higher than carnal thinking. It's inept thinking that leads to false conclusions and perverted thought.

DEVELOPING A SUPERNATURAL LIFESTYLE

Though Elijah lived in the natural world, he operated at the supernatural level, where he saw the invisible and did the impossible. During a time of judgment and catastrophic drought with no food or water, Elijah remained by a beautiful stream, receiving a supernatural supply of food from the ravens. (See 1 Kings 17:1–6.) On another occasion, he was fed by an angel. (See 1 Kings 19:5–8.) The prophet lived in the supernatural realm, and his lifestyle reflected God's power.

Though we still live in this world, we don't have to wait for our future life in heaven because we were meant to live now in the supernatural realm like the prophets. I want to experience it now and reside in the spiritual places of the supernatural.

My wife and I and our beautiful daughter see and live supernaturally here in California. We are blessed, provided for, and guided without others' assistance because our eyes are on the Lord for our help. It is genuinely astonishing how we receive provision and significant breakthroughs.

Praying in the spirit is a powerful way to remain sensitive to this realm of the supernatural. Paul said, *"I thank my God I pray with tongues more than you all"* (1 Corinthians 14:18). In every way, Paul demonstrated how to live supernaturally.

In an interview with the Christian History Institute, New Testament professor Gordon Fee describes the supernatural lifestyle of Paul and the early church:

> In the first century, it was assumed Christians would experience these things. For example, when Paul scolded the Galatians, he began a sentence, "He who richly supplies you with the Spirit and performs miracles in your midst..." Paul spoke in the present tense—the Spirit was dynamically active, doing extraordinary things in Galatia, and the Galatians were well aware of it. He assumed the same common experience when he wrote the church at Corinth.
>
> Now, Paul did have some unusual experiences of the Spirit, but he never made an issue of them. In 2 Corinthians 12, for instance, he mentions having been "caught up to the third heaven," and he seems to be validating his ministry by mentioning this experience.[13]

The early church was a testimony of what it means to live a supernatural lifestyle of miracles, dreams, visions, remarkable healings, and experiences in the heavenly realm. On some occasions, those early Christians didn't know exactly what had happened, but their supernatural ways were the rule, not the exception.

---

13. "The Natural Supernatural," *Christian History* magazine No. 47, "Paul and His Times"; christianhistoryinstitute.org/magazine/article/pauls-natural-supernatural.

ANOTHER CLASS IN HEAVEN

In my vision of heaven, after the class on courage, I was with King David walking toward the beautiful park as we were saying our goodbyes. I continued walking to another part of heaven and came upon door I had not seen before. Looking in, I noticed it was another classroom. I didn't see an angel standing by the door. Even the tables were set up differently than the long tables for the other class.

This classroom was arranged with round tables, evenly spaced, with seats for four people per table. I walked in and sat down, scooting my chair up to the round table. The teacher, who was behind me, started speaking about numbers in the Bible. I swung myself around to see who was talking and immediately thought, *This isn't a class for me, but my grandmother would love it.* Dr. Billye Brim often speaks on eschatology and profound studies of the Bible.

The teacher said that every number in the Bible means something, and there's always a reason for a particular number in each Scripture. As the teacher continued, he told us we would learn about the number eight, and then he distributed a paper to each of us. Glancing at this paper, I noticed the number eight was enormous, almost taking up the whole page with lines on both sides. It seemed that we would be learning to identify each part of the number eight, which had ten pieces to it.

I remember looking at the teacher and taking note of his appearance. He had long, white hair past his shoulders and a long white beard. He was wearing a very loose oversized robe type of outfit, the kind of robe people would have worn thousands of years ago. The teacher was unusually tall at six feet, five inches, with clothes perfectly tailored to him. His robe ended about a half-inch from the ground, and it swayed when he walked.

I knew this teacher had much wisdom and knowledge. In his hand, he carried a huge Bible that was made of wood with gold finishings on each corner. I remember how the other students in this class were busy working on their papers, but I didn't know what to do about the number eight. Even now, if someone gave me the number eight and told me to identify different parts of it, I would still be confused. So, I lifted my hand as the teacher began walking my way from across the room, slowly and calmly holding his Bible close to his chest as he walked. He came over to help me, and I remember him opening his Bible. Suddenly, the vision ended.

THE ANSWERS TO EVERY QUESTION WE NEED HELP WITH ARE ALWAYS DISCOVERED IN THE WORD OF GOD.

The answers to every question we need help with are always discovered in the Word of God. Reflecting on my supernatural visit to heaven, I grasped how important the Word of God was to that teacher and how it needs to be the same for us. Even the way he held his Bible, so close to his chest, made it clear how precious and dear it was to him. The Book must never be thrown on the ground; it must be cherished, and we must realize its importance. We can believe the promises of God and take Him at His Word.

EIGHT—NEW BEGINNING AND A NEW COVENANT

Returning to where I was worshipping God, the first thing I wanted to do was find out what the number eight meant. It means a new beginning. Eight is connected with Jesus and His resurrection, as He was resurrected on the eighth day after He was chosen to be sacrificed for the sins of humanity. Eight people were saved in the ark to continue the human race and reboot humankind, leading to a new beginning.

I knew God was speaking to me that I was on the path of a new beginning. It also means eternal covenant. According to Jewish tradition, Abraham walked in a figure eight around his animal sacrifices to the Lord, resulting in an everlasting covenant. (See Genesis 15:9–21.) His covenant with you and me will never be broken.

This isn't just my new beginning, but yours as well. Your new beginning is a courageous, faith-filled walk with God. Even if you feel like you have missed it or sense it's too late, that is a lie.

Consider these encouraging words in Hebrews 4:16: *"Let us therefore come boldly to the throne of grace, that we may obtain mercy and find grace to help in time of need."* Come boldly without fear into the presence of God, whose throne is grace. That is the only place where you get mercy and the needed grace to assist you in those times when you think you have failed.

From this day forward, walk bravely with God, having confidence that He will open a new beginning in your ministry and walk with Him. I pray that the Holy Spirit ministers to your heart and that God's presence will comfort you and bring the words in this book to your memory. I believe that any hurts or struggles are melting away in Jesus's mighty name from this day forward. Amen.

When Destanie and I moved to our apartment in Hollywood, California, it was a significant step in faith. We knew it was God and trusted Him. The Lord spoke to us about increasing our faith, and we knew there would be hindrances to us if we decided not to move. Our emotions tried to get the best of us, while the enemy put thoughts in our heads, telling us we would run out of money. The enemy flooded our minds with questions like, *What are you going to do? Are you really supposed to be in California?*

We cast those thoughts out of our minds and chose to be led by our spirit, knowing we were doing what God told us to do. The day came when we packed up all of our belongings and started our adventure in Hollywood. We were on the path God had for our lives; we both knew we were obeying Him. As we drove to our new home, we stirred up our faith in God, knowing He was with us. We both had peace as we started this new adventure with God.

We then received a call from Destanie's dad. He said, "I was at the hotel eating breakfast, and a guy came up to me and asked me if my daughter and son-in-law were moving or something." Not knowing the exact day of our move, her dad replied, "I think so." Then, the man responded, "Tell them it will be okay, for God is with them."

What a blessing and confirmation from God this was to us! For God to give us a second confirmation like this encouraged us greatly as we pulled into our new home in Hollywood. As we pulled into our parking garage and approached our assigned parking spot, we saw the number eight. Wow! The Holy Spirit comforted me, and then I remembered the vision about courage and trusting God in our new beginning and how our covenant was with God.

THE POWER OF PRAYER

Now that I was living in Hollywood, God impressed upon me to walk the streets daily, pray, and declare Hollywood for Jesus. I was praying for a mighty outpouring of a move of God to sweep over the dirty, sinful streets. I knew this wouldn't be a long season, but I would do it as long as I lived there, which was two years. I read books about the spiritual history of Hollywood, how prayers impacted the Hollywood Hills, and how the area was once called Holy Wood.

Lester Sumrall used to say that you can tell when God has a special call for a place because Satan goes after it the most. He definitely went after Hollywood the most. Why? Because it has a loud, influential voice. Did we see Hollywood change in the natural like we wanted to when we were living there? No, but we did see many people who we interacted with getting touched by Jesus. We know prayer works. The prayers we sow never go away; they will always bring forth a harvest!

We are seeing our fruit being produced now. California was changing when we launched our bimonthly prayer meetings, with thousands of people from all across the globe tuning in to pray, especially for California. Prayer works and has much power! John Wesley said, "God does nothing but by prayer and everything with it." Billy Graham said the three most important things you can do "are to pray, pray, pray." And prayer was the heartbeat of their missions.

It is a lifestyle we must live by, realizing the utmost importance of spending time in prayer. Living a life of prayer enables you to change your home and even your city. The great revivalist Charles Finney had a prayer partner, Rev. Daniel Nash, also known as Father Nash, who would travel with him for a specific purpose. According to Pastor J. Paul Reno, Nash "would slip quietly into town and seek to get two or three people to enter into a covenant of prayer with him. Sometimes he had with him a man of similar prayer ministry, Abel Clary. Together they would begin to pray fervently for God to move in the community."[14]

Once, Finney was going to minister in Bolton, England, so Nash and Clary sought lodging there. They rented the "dark and damp cellar" of an elderly woman's humble cottage. "In that self-chosen cell, those prayer partners battled the forces of darkness."[15]

What was the key? Prayer! Father Nash was contending with the enemy in the spirit for breakthroughs, and he would get it!

The great missionary and faith healer John G. Lake was on a midnight walk in Mount Tabor Park in Portland, Oregon, when he experienced what became known as "The Portland

---

14. J. Paul Reno, "Daniel Nash 1775-1831 – Prayer Warrior for Charles Finney"; www.hopefaithprayer.com/prayer-warrior-charles-finney. See also: Charles Finney, *Holy Spirit Revivals* (New Kensington, PA: Whitaker House, 1999).
15. Reno, "Daniel Nash 1775-1831 – Prayer Warrior for Charles Finney."

Vision." An angel appeared to Lake, who discerned that the angel's heart was overburdened.

> In answer to this, the angel said, *"Human selfishness and human pride have consumed and dissipated the very glory and heavenly power that God once gave from heaven to this movement as you have beheld tonight."*[16]

Lake asked the angel, *"What constitutes real Pentecost? What ideal should be held before the minds of men as the will of God exhibited through a movement like this?"*

The angel reached for the Bible that Lake was carrying and opened it to the book of Acts.

> He said, *"This is Pentecost as God gave it through the heart of Jesus. Strive for this. Contend for this. Teach the people to pray for this. For this, and this alone, will meet the necessity of the human heart, and this alone will have the power to overcome the forces of darkness."* When the angel was departing, he said, *"Pray. Pray. Pray. Teach the people to pray. Prayer and prayer alone, much prayer, persistent prayer, is the door of entrance into the heart of God."*[17]

I AM A MISSIONARY

Late one night in Hollywood, when Destanie was already asleep, I was up praying, preparing to fly out the next morning to minister, and listening off and on to a minister on TV who was sharing all these powerful stories of being on a mission field. Then, I heard these words, "Branden, you are a missionary

---

16. "The Portland Vision," Healing Rooms Ministries; healingrooms.com/about/johnGLake/?document=107.
17. Ibid.

to California." I felt such a relief knowing God had sent me to California. I was so excited, I woke up Destanie and told her, "God said I'm a missionary to California." She said, "Yes, that's great," and then she went back to sleep.

The next day, on the way to the airport, I received a call from the pastor where I was speaking the following day. He had been praying and felt led to tell me, "You are a missionary to California." With excitement, I told him what I had heard the night before, and the pastor said, "This is the Holy Spirit confirming it with you now."

What is a missionary? It comes from the word "apostle," which means "sent one." Wherever you live, you are sent by God. Knowing this will give you the courage to pray and watch your city or town be changed by God's presence.

WHEREVER YOU LIVE, YOU ARE SENT BY GOD. KNOWING THIS WILL GIVE YOU THE COURAGE TO PRAY AND WATCH YOUR CITY OR TOWN BE CHANGED BY GOD'S PRESENCE.

To be honest with you, I still believe in God for the courage I need; it's nothing you master but something you receive from Him. A person of courage is also full of faith. Walt Disney said that all our dreams come true if we dare to pursue them.

We need courage daily. I need to sense God's presence daily, even after hearing the Lord tell me, "I've called you as a missionary to California." Even after some time had gone by, I questioned myself.

One time in a prayer meeting, I was asked to share, so I felt compelled to share about being a missionary to California. When I said that, the power of God hit me like a punch in the gut with such force that I couldn't move or speak one word in front of everyone. As I walked away, each foot was frozen in the air with every step! It was like the Lord was telling me, "Don't ever question what I've told you. I challenge you never to allow the enemy to question what I say to you and not let the enemy discourage you."

You are now stepping in and living your new beginning with a covenant-keeping God who will not break His covenant. Make it your prayer and aim always to have courage no matter what! Your new courageous life starts now.

ENCOUNTERING HIS LOVE

Most of humanity has heard about Jesus and heaven. Heaven is a real place where we will spend eternity. You have read a little about my visions of the two classes, but there is still so much more I didn't see. Other people have seen and shared stories about the different parts of heaven. One of my spiritual fathers, Dr. Gary Wood, is now in heaven for the second time. The first time he went, when he was eighteen, he saw his own beautiful mansion and even went inside it. Its walls were white, but there were buckets of paint on the floor. Wood threw a bucket of paint against the wall, which created a beautiful floral scene, and a wonderful fragrance filled the room.

Heaven is our true home, and the only way you can get there is by knowing Jesus as your Lord and Savior. In John 14:6, Jesus said, "*I am the way, the truth, and the life. No one comes to the Father except through Me.*"

Some people have different interpretations of Jesus, some from past hurt or wrong interpretations of Scripture. Whatever the reason, they genuinely don't know who Jesus is.

Jesus is love beyond your ability to even begin to describe Him. His beauty is breathtaking, and He is awesome and all-knowing. His eyes project love and compassion overflowing into your heart. His smile awakens and inspires you.

Encountering Jesus and knowing His love for you will completely change your life. Though your heart may be calloused and somewhat cold, the moment you discover His love for the first time, it will melt your heart forever, and nothing else will matter to you except Jesus.

I love my wife and daughter with all my heart, but Jesus is my number one. I long for Him daily and find myself sacrificing sleep sometimes because I want to worship and be with Him. He is my life, and my life is His.

Walking in courage requires trusting God, not walking in your strength or abilities or even this book. Those who are strong have a revelation of Jesus and His love for us. Knowing He lives inside us makes us bold and courageous without any effort.

Jesus lived his earthly life empowered and nourished by His Father's love for Him.

If you keep my commands, you will live in my love, just as I have kept my Father's commands, for I continually live nourished and empowered by his love. (John 15:10 TPT)

Jesus wasn't affected by criticism or even by the praise from His disciples, but He was consumed by His Father's love, which was His daily nourishment.

Jesus was always going off by Himself to pray so that He could spend time alone in the presence of His Father, enjoying His love, nourished by His presence, and empowered to do His Father's will. Jesus was always in perfect harmony with the Father's intentions. The word "nourish" means to provide someone with food. God's love was Jesus's food, and it can be ours as well. When His love fills us, it results in a courageous lifestyle.

Every year, we preach on a tour across the beautiful country of Canada. We travel for around twenty days from the west to the east as well as the north. The last tour we did was nonstop and lasted till we got to Toronto. Many of the churches were not very large. I was always asked, "Where are you preaching next?" I would mention that our last stop was at this particular church in Toronto, and everyone always said, "That's a big church."

BREAKING LIFE'S SPEED CONTROL

I didn't think much of this till we got to Toronto and checked into our hotel. I received an email explaining the itinerary at the Sunday morning service. It listed how many songs there would be and how long I was allotted to preach, which was around twenty-five minutes. If I'm preaching somewhere I have never preached before, I already know what message I will speak. I always share my testimony of how God gave me a message to preach about the name of Jesus.

It's a message the devil hates. He doesn't want Christians to know about the power we have in the name of Jesus because it gives us authority over him. The devil doesn't mind you singing about the name of Jesus, but when someone understands that power and knows how to speak the name of Jesus with passion and faith, then the enemy trembles.

I arrived on Sunday morning to meet with the pastor, and then we began to walk out to the service in the auditorium, where thousands of people were waiting. Wow, it was a big church! I went to my seat in the front row, waiting to preach, and as the worship music was playing, I was deeply touched by God's love. The lyrics and the music coming from the instruments penetrated me, and God's love nourished me. I began to cry as the presence of God filled the room.

Trying to pull myself together, I started to think about all the courageous decisions I had made in my life to arrive at that place. I sensed God's pleasure as I was weeping; I thought to myself, *Branden, get yourself together, for you are about to preach.* Just then, God told me, "Break the speed control in your life." I thought, *What speed control is in my life?*

While I was pondering this, I thought about driving on a highway. Your speed limit might be sixty-five miles an hour, depending on which state you are in. If you set your car's cruise control to sixty-five, you can maintain the appropriate rate of speed without fluctuating up or down.

Applying this message spiritually, I knew that I put my life with God on heavenly speed control, allowing God to touch my life and use me at whatever speed He pleased. I had completely surrendered to Him.

> *Let this mind be in you which was also in Christ Jesus, who,*
> *being in the form of God, did not consider it robbery to be*
> *equal with God, but made Himself of no reputation, taking*
> *the form of a bondservant, and coming in the likeness of*
> *men. And being found in appearance as a man, He hum-*
> *bled Himself and became obedient to the point of death,*
> *even the death of the cross. Therefore God also has highly*
> *exalted Him and given Him the name which is above every*
> *name.* (Philippians 2:5–9)

These compelling verses must be applied to our own lives. Notice the prophetic language in these words: He *"made Himself of no reputation,"* took *"the form of a bondservant," "humbled Himself"* to appear as a Man, and was *"obedient to the point of death"* on the cross.

Jesus surrendered Himself without exception, doing the will of His Father and dying on the cross for us. Jesus broke every limit to allow God to use Him. He laid it all down for you and me to accomplish His Father's will.

At the service in Toronto, the Holy Spirit said, "Branden, if I decide to undo you in His presence and love, in front of people, let Me." As soon as God spoke, I heard the pastor calling me up to preach. While heading to the platform, I began to share a few words and then ran back up to the podium and said, "No time limit. The anointing of God is here this morning."

We had a great move of God in that service! The pastor called every young person to the front for me to minister to them and set them ablaze with God's fire. And that evening, we had another service!

BE WHO YOU WERE MEANT TO BE

We can live a life so nourished and empowered by God's love that it breaks every speed control we have set. This allows the love of God that has been shed abroad in our hearts to flow through us so we can impact the world around us. In this way, we break the sound barrier into the presence of God and speak His language, the language of love!

The evangelist Leonard Ravenhill once said that three people live inside each of us: the one who we think we are; the one who others think we are; and the one God knows we are. When you are the person God created you to be, you live in a place of peace and rest in God's love. Anything else is a counterfeit.

Don't try to be someone you are not through an outward performance or a religious duty. Throw away the fake self and move into a relationship with Jesus to experience love like you never imagined.

THROW AWAY THE FAKE SELF AND MOVE INTO A RELATIONSHIP WITH JESUS TO EXPERIENCE LOVE LIKE YOU NEVER IMAGINED.

Relationships often end because of jealous conflicts, and jealousy can even lead to murder. Look at the life of King Saul.

There was a time when Saul had his eyes on God, but when David killed Goliath, the whole town was cheering for David, saying, *"Saul has slain his thousands, and David his ten thousands"* (1 Samuel 18:7). From that day on, Saul kept a close, jealous eye on David. (See verse 9.) Saul had enjoyed living in the limelight and being number one in the people's eyes, but now, Saul's insecurity made him angry enough to try to kill the young hero.

Comparing yourself to others is a quick trip to nowhere because you were never supposed to be them; you are God's unique creation, one of a kind. In this technological age, the hook of jealousy and envy, though natural, entangles you in a web of social media that is only prepared to amp it up. Followers and likes appear to be solid proof of a person's value—but don't take the bait. Don't try to impress the world by imitating others and comparing yourself to them. Instead, imitate God and be who He called you to be.

It's not just in the world of teenagers; it's also in the world of preachers and ministers. I love my grandmother, and she has been incredibly successful in ministry, but I don't try to replicate her or minister in her style. Why? It's not me or my calling.

On one occasion when I was preaching at a church, God moved massively in the service. My family wasn't there in person but was watching it online. My brother Jared told my mom, "It's amazing how Branden is up there, not trying to impress people or be something he's not but just himself."

I'm not sharing this to illustrate my point that being ourselves is a critical step in the right direction. After I heard what Jared said, the Lord told me, "I can't anoint anyone who is inauthentic; I anoint authenticity." Isn't that powerful? When we are just ourselves, we glow like the stars destined by God's design to help others in our unique way.

The number one reason other Christians have hurt people is that they encounter Christians who were not authentic, who were hurt and frustrated with themselves being something they are not. When you know who you are, loved by the Father, you can just be you, and then God's love flows like a river through you to others without effort.

Courage doesn't come from having a strong personality like the alpha dog in a pack. Courage comes when we learn from Jesus, who lived the ultimate, authentic, courageous life.

Take My yoke upon you and learn from Me, for I am gentle and lowly in heart, and you will find rest for your souls.
(Matthew 11:29)

Jesus was the ultimate teacher. Unlike the religious leaders of His day, who were harsh, overbearing, and oppressive, Jesus taught by being meek, mild, and gentle in His leadership. Courage is not necessarily for the physically strong but for the brave. In the words of Mark Twain, "It is curious—curious that physical courage should be so common in the world, and moral courage so rare."

Courage is not only found on the battlefield but also in less obvious places. Pastor Charles Swindoll made a great point when he said, "Courage is not limited to the battlefield or the Indianapolis 500 or bravely catching a thief in your house. The real tests of courage are much quieter. They are the inner tests, like remaining faithful when nobody's looking, like enduring pain when the room is empty, like standing alone when you're misunderstood." To see what is right and to do it—now that is courage.

In life, we have to make choices that require us to be courageous without being discouraged. Each day, when we face tough decisions, we can trust God and choose courage or shrink away from them. I have learned the empowering force of God's love and grace, which makes us appear to be bigger than we are.

David was smaller than the giant Goliath, but he lived a courageous life, having such a love for God that it empowered and nourished him in the toughest of times. We are called to be like an oil lamp, not hidden under a basket but letting the heavenly light burn brightly in the world. (See Matthew 5:14–16.) To maintain the fire of God in your life, you must fill your oil lamp, so your light doesn't flicker and die. The Word of God and worship is the necessary oil you need to keep your light burning in a darkened world.

You can't give what you don't have—living an overflowing life from the presence of God is required to have something to share with others. When you fill a glass with water to overflowing, everything is affected around you. Be filled to overflowing with living water.

> Jesus stood and cried out, saying, "If anyone thirsts, let him come to Me and drink. He who believes in Me, as the Scripture has said, out of his heart will flow rivers of living water." (John 7:37–38)

And in 1 Corinthians 12:13, we are told to drink of one Spirit, the everlasting water. We must live a life like that cup overflowing, and from the overflow, courage will come like an unceasing tide that impacts those who come to the water. "*Come, all you who are thirsty, come to the waters*" (Isaiah 55:1 NIV). We can't give out anything we don't have. We need the Word of God and worship to fill our lamps with oil and the living water that is Jesus to spill out of our glasses so we can share His love with the world.

Living life in a secret place with Jesus changed my life forever. It all started with me crying out to God in the most challenging times, asking for courage to make the right and necessary choices, and then making the right decisions. Daily delighting in the Lord and feeding on His love have sustained me in my everyday activities.

You can do what I did, for it only takes a little courage to make the right decisions if you lean on Him for strength and support. You were never meant to live a meaningless life because God is your life. You are a masterpiece created by God to courageously work for His glory and start your new beginning.

ABOUT THE AUTHOR

Branden Brim is a full-time minister and the founder of His Name Ministries, based on Acts 3:16. He and his wife Destanie launched the ministry after the Lord gave Branden a message about the name of Jesus and the power in His name.

Branden previously worked alongside his grandmother, Dr. Billye Brim of Billye Brim Ministries, to spread and preach the gospel throughout the world.

Branden's passion is to see people touched by the power of God and realize the power of Jesus's name. He ministers with a strong word, anointed worship, and gifts of healing.

He has appeared on a variety of media platforms, including Trinity Broadcast Network (TBN) and *The Prophetic Witness* television show. He is a regular on the radio show *The Voice of One Witness* with Dr. Billye Brim.

Branden is also the Internet and TV host for Autumn Assembly, attended by thousands of people from Missouri and beyond. He has been a guest speaker at many conferences and churches, including Hillsong Church LA and Christ for the Nations Bible School.

He and his family currently reside in Southern California.